For the love of Marje

A moving story of love, loss and the fight against cancer.

Swasie Turner MBE

JEREMY MILLS
PUBLISHING LIMITED

**This book is dedicated to the treasured memory
of my dear wife Marjorie.**

Published by Jeremy Mills Publishing Limited
www.jeremymillspublishing.co.uk

First Published 2007

ISBN 978-1-905217-28-1

Contents

FOR THE LOVE OF MARJE

Sponsor's Welcome

Sunrise Medical is one of the world's largest manufacturers of homecare and extended care products. Founded in 1983, the Sunrise Medical family of products has been built from many of the most popular brands in the home care industry including Quickie, Lomax, Breezy, Jay, Coopers, and Sterling. We operate manufacturing facilities in the United Kingdom, Mexico, the United States, Germany, and Spain and our products are distributed to suppliers through dedicated sales organizations and distributors in over 90 countries worldwide.

Sunrise's goal is to improve the lives of the people who use our products. When you know every effort in your day directly affects the lives of others, you become a company made up of individuals who try harder, work smarter and who have come to understand the true value of innovation. Our products are designed to promote independent and involved lifestyles. They are about abilities, and are dedicated to quality of design and its impact on the quality of life.

Sunrise actively supports members of the disabled community through its Ambassador programme. Our Ambassadors include disabled athletes and other prominent people who through their work and attitude make a significant difference to the physical and mental well being of the disabled.

Sunrise are proud to be associated with Swasie Turner, an individual whose tireless charity work benefits so many.

For more information on Sunrise Medical or its products, visit our website at www.sunrisemedical.com

Preface

Due to the horrific injuries the author sustained as the result of a gratuitous act of violence while serving as a front line police officer, his life-changing scenario and its aftermath are candidly related in this 'no holds barred' illustrated publication. His injuries were such that it was necessary to amputate his right leg high above the knee. Adapting to a wheelchair and having to accept his new life 'on the seat of his pants' as well as the loss of his beloved career, further tragedy was to befall him. Only nine short months after returning home from hospital, Swasie then suffered the inconsolable loss of his wife and lifelong sweetheart Marjorie, to the scourge of cancer.

Totally heartbroken, Swasie eventually managed to pull himself up and decided to go all out to assist the fight against the relentless killer that had stolen his wife. His obsessive efforts and endeavours to come to terms with his predicament will hopefully be an incentive and inspiration to others.

Swasie does not pull any punches as he relates, in his own words, his constant irritation regarding those in wheelchairs being treated as though they are second-class citizens. People tend to regard them as 'not being present' when conversing with their companions or carers, and being spoken about – but not to! These same people, according to the author, tend to assume that because people are in wheelchairs, irrespective of their age, physical or mental condition or capabilities, they are unable to grasp even the simplest of situations or appreciate what is going on around them.

This book describes in graphic detail the pitfalls and attitudes towards and treatment of those who are physically handicapped. Travelling on through the pages makes extremely interesting and sometimes controversial reading as Swasie takes issue with the many 'Jobsworths' he encountered. Also highlighted is the attitude by a generally able-bodied society towards those who are physically handicapped.

Foreword

By Fiona Castle OBE, widow of the late Roy Castle,
the world's true master of mirth

Swasie Turner's honest account of some very traumatic events in his life makes compelling reading. He is a giant of a man with a big heart and steely determination.

He spares neither himself nor others, his honest appraisal of human behaviour. This must be very helpful to many who are going through difficult circumstances in life. He says, quite rightly, that people respond to traumas in different ways and there's no right way, but rather a variety of ways to cope. He confesses to depression, self pity and even thoughts of suicide after the death of his beloved wife. But with great courage he overcomes his grief by devoting himself to fundraising and earth-stattering feats of courage, in defiance of his injuries. As a result, many charities are the beneficiaries of the money raised from his amazing and creative achievements.

This is an inspiring and moving story which I am sure will encourage any reader to take hold of life and make the most of every moment. What an example Swasie is to us all.

CHAPTER ONE

Catastrophic Life Change

Life was going well for me as a police sergeant as I carried out my daily duties. Each day brought a new adventure or two as I diligently sleuthed out and about along the bustling streets of Wallasey, Merseyside. I had enjoyed my 27 years of service as a front line police officer which had included eight years in the CID, 'active service' as a firearms officer, Vice Squad and eventually I reached the dizzy heights of a PSU (Police Support Unit) commander. My posting from Liverpool 'over the water' to Wallasey was Utopia. Being born and bred in Saughall Massie on the Wirral, my Wallasey posting was only a couple of miles from my home. As a section sergeant, I was blessed with a fine selection of officers under my command and life in general was fine.

There had been a 'fly in the ointment' due to a previous scare we experienced a year before, when my wife Marjorie had undergone a lumpectomy for breast cancer. This was done privately to facilitate speed. After the op all went well and Marje was constantly supervised and monitored as she responded well to her post-operative treatment and prescribed medication. Thankfully, she was now almost in remission and things seemed to be getting back to normal.

Marje and I had been together from when we were fourteen year-old childhood sweethearts. Our subsequent marriage was blessed with two children; our son Ron (who also became a police officer) and our daughter Joanne. As the wife of a front line police officer, Marje had many times suffered the trauma of her husband being injured on numerous occasions but, as always, she had coped well. During such traumatic times she was my total pillar of strength.

Swasie as Patrol Sergeant (late 1980s).

Marje and Swasie's Wedding day, 26th July 1958.

She had coped equally well in similar circumstances during my previous five-year career as a firefighter with Cheshire County Fire Brigade.

Marje enjoyed her work as the manageress of a local cake shop and by and large, even after nearly 40 years, we were both without doubt still under the anaesthetic of 'matrimonial enchantment'!

However, our domestic bliss was to be brought to a devastating halt by an act of deliberate and gratuitous violence which would change the lives of me and my family forever.

Whilst out on a routine foot patrol one day, accompanied by one of my young constables in the seaside resort of New Brighton,

I heard the sound of an approaching high-powered motorcycle travelling at speed. I stepped out into the roadway and signalled the rider to stop. The machine slowed down and appeared to be stopping. I approached the rider with the intention of chastising him for the manner in which he was driving his machine at speed in a crowded and built up area, then I would check him and his machine. Thinking the driver was about to pull in I walked towards him. Being now a short distance away, the rider suddenly engaged a lower gear, revved his 1,200cc engine and accelerated violently, lifting his front wheel off the ground as he shot forward. The rider aimed his Kawasaki machine directly at me which then struck me violently sending me into the air and throwing me some distance along the road. I landed in a crumpled and broken heap, suffering acute pain to my right side, my right knee having taken the brunt of the impact. Amazingly, the rider mounted the pavement and scattered a nearby bus queue before driving back onto the road and on through a set of traffic lights showing red and making good his escape.

My injuries were such that I would need fourteen operations which would include two knee replacements to my shattered right leg. These operations were to be of no avail however, and subsequently my right leg had to be amputated high above the knee.

Having participated in martial arts, boxing and weightlifting for most of my adult life, this was absolutely devastating. Not only did it cause the premature demise of my beloved police career, but it also put paid to my activities in the gym and the boxing club. I was truly shattered and thought the end of my physical world had come with a depressing and self-pitying vengeance.

My world had well and truly fallen apart. I remember clearly the day I went into hospital for the 'big chop', the inevitable amputation of my right leg. I had already lost half of my right hand due to a ferocious attack from a burglar's large Alsatian dog when I arrested his master for breaking into a shop. Although I had managed to hang on to my job by a hair's breadth that time, my career had well and truly evaporated due to the latest incident in New Brighton. Marje and my daughter Jo sat alongside my bed after my admission to ward C-M 4 at Clatterbridge Hospital in Bebington, Wirral, the day before my operation. We were all very emotional but it was then, as I looked at my treasured wife, that I suddenly realised just how extremely lucky I was! I looked at my wife, the very lady who had bravely suffered the terrifying trauma of having to accept being diagnosed with breast cancer. I clearly remembered reassuring *her* on receiving her own devastating news, telling her that all would turn out okay as I dabbed her tearful eyes a year or so before.

This time however, it was my extremely brave and comforting wife who was reassuring *me* that all would be okay! The large lump in my throat almost choked me as I realised and appreciated the fact that I still had my wife after such a 'near miss'. I was upset also as I looked at my darling daughter who encouraged me by uttering her own comforting sentiments. Eventually, Marje and Jo rose to leave me. Marje leaned over to kiss me goodbye until the following day, and Jo did likewise. The next time that I would see them both I would be minus my leg! I couldn't believe how things had turned from a comparatively normal, simple but happy way of life into a heartbreaking and traumatic, life-altering scenario.

Due to the following day's surgery I could only have a cup of tea that evening. I received a message from the ward sister later that night saying that Marje had rung last thing to again wish me well for the following day. I was unable to sleep at first and tossed and turned as I tried to enter the bliss of slumber land, but such a luxury evaded me. Eventually I managed to doze fitfully and the night dragged on until the morning nursing shift came on duty. No tea this time; 'Nil by mouth'! as the instructive note said at the head of my bed. As the time went on and activity increased, I received visits from various doctors and physiotherapists. Finally, I was prepped for theatre. My lower torso and right leg were shaved after which copious amounts of iodine were slopped all over the shaved area, stinging where the razor had been pedantically and expertly used by the extremely competent nurse. Finally, I was wrapped in an envelope of green surgical covering ready for my op. After lying there for what seemed to be an eternity, staring at the ceiling and letting my thoughts run riot, I was collected by the porter with his reassuring banter which he had no doubt practised over a long period to perfection! Soon, I would be sent off to sleep to undergo the operation. After the needle was skilfully and painlessly inserted into the vein on the back of my left hand and the mask was placed over my face, I rapidly descended into the dark, bottomless pit of deep anaesthesia.

Hours later, as the nauseating oblivion of my anaesthetic started to fade, slowly allowing my re-entry into the *real* world, I could hear the distant sound of rattling tea cups and cutlery. I then heard the soothing, reassuring voice of a female; she was mentioning my name! I felt someone gently take hold of my hand, 'Come on, wake up Mr Turner, you're alright now, it's all over'! I tried to remember where the hell I was and what was going on. I tried to move but my feeble effort brought a sudden, extremely sharp stab of pain that engulfed the whole of my groin area. I heard myself yell out loudly and profanely and I felt as though I was going to be violently sick. I felt hands holding me and again I heard the pleasant, dulcet tones of the lady's voice, this time very close. 'Everything's okay now, don't try to move, just lie still and I'll get you something for the pain'.

Although I still had difficulty lifting my head, the excruciating pain in my groin and upper thigh area brought me quickly to some sense of reality. I became acutely aware now that I'd been to theatre and realised that I'd had an operation on my damaged leg. My left foot was cold and the 'phantom' toes of my non-existent right foot were giving me painful pins and needles. I tried to move my right leg and again the excruciating pain caused me to yell and curse out loud.

There were now a couple of nurses and a doctor by my bed. They all tried (unsuccessfully) to help adjust me into a more comfortable position. My pillow was patted and I was painfully moved further up the bed. I opened my eyes and tried to focus my blurred vision.

I saw, but couldn't accept, that the bulge of only one leg, my left, showed under the bed covers. Beyond the 'cage' protecting my extremely short stump there was just a flat area where my right leg should be. I must have been in senior officer mode as my brain could not interpret or explain to me why the blanket was flat. I felt very groggy and a nurse appeared with a mug of hot sweet tea. She helped me as I slowly sipped the most welcome nectar. Tears welled in my eyes before rolling down my cheeks as I suddenly realised the gravity of my situation – my right leg! Bloody hell, they've taken it off! 'Jesus Christ, what the *hell* am I going to do now?' The ever comforting 'Florence Nightingale' placed an arm around my shoulder and whispered, 'You *will* cope, I *know* you will!' Self pity swept through me and engulfed my whole being. This then turned into anger at the thought of my dilemma having been brought about by a bloody thug, a piece of low life scum who had deliberately injured me so badly that they had to amputate my right leg high above the knee. How I hated the bastard responsible for crippling me, and how I wished him all the harm in the world. My hatred was such that I could (and definitely would) have damaged him seriously had I been in a position to do so. I felt *very* bitter; how was I going to get through this? I had always been very physical; weightlifting, boxing and regular training in the gym had until now been my way of life and had been almost a religion to me.

There was also the thought as to how I would be able to look after my darling Marje. All these things filled my now, very troubled mind alongside the overwhelming feeling of self pity that was totally consuming me.

After a subsequent visit by my surgeon to check all was well, I was heavily sedated and a 'wrist watch' was fitted to my wrist. This was in fact an ingenious item which, at a press of the dial, would administer a shot of pain-killing morphine. I drifted in and out of delirious consciousness for a couple of hours or so. Now and again I heard voices as doctors and nurses constantly visited my bed to check me over.

Marje and Swasie engaged at seventeen (1957).

Later, I was woken by a gentle kiss on my forehead and I heard the warm, comforting and dulcet tone of my Marje who announced her arrival with her usual, 'Hi Love, it's only me'. I opened my eyes to see her and Jo at my bedside. My pain was excruciating but seeing Marje and feeling her squeezing my hand was the best tonic I could ever have wished for. Although they were both obviously very upset at the final outcome of my criminal injury, it was poor Jo who could not hold back the tears and she cried uncontrollably when she saw the give-away flat area of my bed sheet. Marje too was visibly upset but, being my pillar of strength, my rock, as she *always* was, she managed to retain her composure and self control. She gently squeezed my hand and gave me another kiss on the cheek. I knew that *whatever* the future held, I would always have my Marje alongside me so that we could both fight any adversity together as we always had since we started courting and on throughout our 40 years of marriage. The dangers and injuries and the trials and tribulations I had endured during my service in the Fire Brigade and then with the Police Force had given Marje a hard time and some anxious moments on many occasions. I had been hospitalised due to injury many times over the years, but Marje had *always* been there when I needed her. It is definitely the case that the spouse suffers too when they have to tend and comfort their other half as they recover from injury. Marje had suffered in silence during those traumatic times.

As the days went by her regular visits were a tonic. I slowly made progress thanks to the daily visits and instruction I received from the physiotherapists (or physio*terrorists* as I was to jokingly label them). Although they were very sympathetic, they were nevertheless equally determined; their dedicated professionalism knew no bounds. I remain *totally* indebted and profusely grateful to those wonderful doctors, nurses, physiotherapists, tea ladies and cleaners, *all* of whom are of equal importance to ensure the smooth running of a hospital. This in turn maintains the morale and well-being of patients who are trying to come to terms with their lot. Especially those suffering from whimpish self pity like myself!

A couple of days before I was allowed home I was taken to the hospital's limb centre. There, I exercised relentlessly and we tried various types of prosthetics but sadly these attempts proved to be ultimately unsuccessful. During one of my later visits to the centre, I met a man who was an amputee. He just couldn't wait to enlighten me, that 'Yer'll never get used to losin' yer leg son. I 'aven't, an' I lost mine *nine years ago*'! In my state of depression at my own loss that was all I needed to hear! I desperately wanted to get the hell out of there. I didn't want to be with cripples in wheelchairs! – of course, I was completely overlooking the fact that I too was now a member of the very same club! I beat a hasty retreat from such a 'Job's comforter' and decided that I'd keep away from the likes of him in future!

Although I was still experiencing constant post-operative pain and I was not eating very much, I was still undergoing intensive physiotherapy. This did help me along but I was continually experiencing difficulty maintaining my balance. I needed constant assistance and monitoring, as I would easily fall when getting in and out of my bed or using the toilet due to the missing weight of my amputated limb. My predicament was vividly brought home to me when I was placed into my new wheelchair. I immediately resented people pushing me about as *I* needed to be in control. I was fully aware that each and every person who assisted me had my interests and welfare at heart, however, from the very start, I wanted to push myself.

Also, I hated the fact that from now on I would have to look *up* to everyone, as I realised that although I was once a six footer, I was now reduced to a three foot sixer! I was totally in despair as to what my future now held; how on earth was I going to cope? Only time would tell. Thank God I would have my beloved Marje to look after me.

Prior to my hospital discharge I was taken home by nurses from the limb centre. Although my pre-discharge home visit was essential to assess my domestic capabilities, I nevertheless felt humiliation when I was asked to demonstrate to them how I would manage in

Swasie's kitchen.

the kitchen and bathroom. I was requested to show if I could use the bath and the now specially adapted toilet as well as being asked to demonstrate if I could open cupboard doors and drawers. The seriousness of the situation was brought home to me when I was asked to show if I could fill a kettle and boil its contents without scalding myself. All these minor and humdrum things, which are trivial tasks to the able-bodied, were now a totally different physical scenario to me. After satisfying my hospital mentors that I would not be a domestic liability and health hazard, we returned to my ward where I could now prepare myself for my return home in a couple of days' time.

Eventually the day came when I was allowed to go home. I bade those fantastic nurses, doctors and ward staff an emotional farewell and thanked them for their kind ministerings and highly professional and dedicated care. As I was wheeled from the ward and placed into the ambulance, I once again experienced severe frustration as my wheelchair was locked to the floor of the vehicle. I felt like a prisoner and that my life had taken a turn for the worse. What a bloody awful way for things to end up! On arriving home I was warmly greeted by my devoted, close knit family. It was a very emotional return. Marje bent down and gave me a big hug and a welcome home kiss. Jo and Ron also gave me a reassuring and welcoming hug. Again I felt sheer frustration at being pushed down my own path and into the house. Marje remarked that we would have to get a ramp to the door because of the high step, yet *another* obstacle I hadn't thought about. Once inside the house Marje gave me another hug and soon furnished me with a most welcome cup of tea. Marje and my lovely daughter had also been very busy during my absence! They had both been hard at work painting and decorating the house as a surprise for my return. This had all been done just for me; I was so humbled at their efforts it brought tears to my eyes. Within days of returning home I suffered my first horrendous fall. Thinking I had two legs I rose out of my chair and tried to close the sliding conservatory doors. Leaning over to my right I suddenly realised that I didn't have a leg on that side. Consequently I went crashing into the glass doors; how on earth they didn't shatter at my weight hitting them I will never know. The fall caused heavy weeping from my stump scar. This fall also enhanced my already acute lack of morale and confidence. I felt I would *never* get used to being minus my leg.

CHAPTER TWO

Life on the Seat of my Pants

Although throughout my life I had been a keen enthusiast of the gym to maintain a lifestyle of fitness, I nevertheless found at first, getting used to pushing a 47lb standard NHS wheelchair was not the easiest way to get about. I found pushing over thick carpets to be especially hard as the pile was so 'unfriendly' to the casters, which made it hard going. Being blessed with having a fair amount of upper body strength and reasonably strong arms, I thought I would be able to manage without much effort. How wrong I was! I found that propelling my new front castered 'chariot', up even *minor* gradients, was certainly a daunting task.

I was advised by the medics to 'take things easy' for the first twelve months or so to allow the results of my injuries, and ultimate surgery, to heal and settle. However, from the very outset, I wanted to somehow raise funds for Cancer Research in any way I could. This was to express my deep gratitude to those responsible for my Marje having been saved from the cruel clutches of the dreaded disease.

From the start, I was determined to push my wheelchair myself; I was *not* going to be pushed by anyone else if I could help it. Although I did find things difficult at first, my stubborn pig-headedness eventually started to pay dividends as I slowly started getting used to 'flying the machine' solo! Very soon it was brought home to me that pushing myself along the pavements would definitely have to be a 'no no'. I found that the pavements were always liberally covered with copious amounts of filth. This included the extremely offensive results of people indiscriminately spitting everywhere, as well as the ever-present disease ridden deposits from

Swasie out on the icy roads.

our friends in the canine world. These nauseating and infectious substances would impregnate the surface of my tyres before then being transferred onto my hands. This offensive material would then be transferred onto the carpets in my house on my return home. Also, there were broken paving flags and cracks for the casters to fall into, stopping the chair dead. This sometimes resulted in my departure from the chair and a painful dumping onto the ground. I found too that the majority of the kerbsides at junctions or gateways did not drop down flush with the road surface. This makes crossing from one pavement to another at road junctions and mounting the opposite pavements risky. I therefore decided that using the pavements would be non-negotiable! – I would use the roads.

I fitted a mirror to my chair (kindly donated by Bob Jones Motor Cycles of Birkenhead) to ensure my safety by enabling me to be aware of other vehicles on the road. This would hopefully minimise the risk of invoking the wrath of motorists. Contrary to such expectation of impatience from irate motorists I was pleased to find the opposite. I quickly began to experience friendly greetings via their hand waves and horn beeping as they passed me by. This was indeed a pleasant surprise, and gave me the incentive to continue my endeavours with utmost vigour. What started as pushes of two or three miles or so each day soon manifested themselves into distances beyond ten miles. At first I tried to conceal my daily marathon wanderings from the regular visits of my physiotherapist and my wonderful GP Dr Marion Smethurst. I am certainly blessed with having a fantastic GP who continually strives to ensure that all is well with her 'flock'. I would certainly have been scolded by my medical mentors if they had been aware of my physically demanding routine so early after my hospital discharge!

My presence out on the roads, and the reason for my presence, started to become well-known in the area. My daily pushes started to become nocturnal also. I added a horn and obligatory front and rear cycle lights to my chair to cater for 'night sorties'. I also had fitted a cycle mileometer so that a record could be kept of my daily mileage. As the local populace became aware of my endeavours, motorists began to pull in ahead of me before getting out to hand me generous sums of money for 'my' Clatterbridge Hospital Cancer Charity. Some of these people were quite emotional, stating that they too were encountering, or had encountered, cancer in their families. As I steadily became more adept and confident in my new world on the seat of my pants, Marje continued to get better and better after the removal of the cancerous growth from her breast. Believe it or not, the loss of my leg was now taking a back seat, as the most important thing was the good health of my wife; that was paramount. I deemed that it was now *my* turn to devotedly look after *her*, ensuring that her progress and good health continued unabated.

As time went on, my wheelchair-pushing journeys of at least ten miles per day and my fundraising continued to increase. I was now becoming well-known as a 'prolific' fundraiser for Cancer Research at one of Britain's two major cancer research establishments, namely Clatterbridge Hospital. This was the same hospital that was treating Marje and efficiently maintaining her progress. My deep and sincere loyalty to this establishment and its tireless and highly professional research staff will remain with me forever. I deemed Marje's health, progress and welfare to be my main priority, which totally paled my own predicament into insignificance.

Although the people I met on my travels were friendly, considerate and benevolent, my pushes were not totally without incident. Early one morning I was near the end of a twelve-mile push when a white car drew alongside me. I thought it was another donor so I stopped. To my amazement, I heard swearing and cursing and even threats from the car's occupants, which were three young men and a woman. All appeared to be high on drugs. I saw that all the windows of the vehicle were down and suddenly, a glass bottle was thrown at me by a male sitting in the rear seat. The bottle was heading for my face but I deflected and it smashed against my metal chair, covering me in broken glass and its sticky liquid contents, which appeared to be orange cordial. All in the vehicle fell about laughing, then, after more curses and threats, the car drove off at speed. I informed the police of the incident but the yobs responsible were never found. Perhaps they were some of the 'low life' I had dealt with in the past during my police service? If they were, it was obvious that I had not endeared myself to them. I would certainly have liked to have had a word with the bottle thrower!

One day, a chance remark by someone drew my attention to a local, annual event, known as the Wirral Coastal Walk. The event is a fifteen-mile trek from Secombe Ferry in Wallasey, along the coastline around the top of the Wirral peninsular and on to

Thurstastson, the final destination, on the banks of the river Dee. It is for participants to raise money for various charities of their choice. Their combined efforts raise many thousands of pounds for good and worthy causes each year. The lengthy distance included the negotiation of steps, stiles, a sandy stretch of shoreline and narrow footpaths alongside, and across, many fields. I decided to become the first wheelchair to take part in this event to raise money for Clatterbridge Cancer Research. My application was at first received with sceptical apprehension as it was deemed extremely unlikely that I would succeed. The stiles, long grass and narrow paths were not at all 'wheelchair friendly'. However, the powers that be did appreciate my dogged determination. I insisted that I be allowed to take part and finally those in charge courteously (but reluctantly) granted my application. The push was indeed very stamina-sapping and strength-consuming. However, my constant road work paid dividends and I managed to complete the event and raise not only some much needed funds but also the attention of the local press, radio and in turn, television. This turn of events started to prove invaluable. Publicity enhances one's efforts, which breeds notoriety, which then generates the much sought after funds to fill the coffers. I paid a penalty for 'showing off' during this cross country marathon when, nearing the end of the fifteen miles, I spotted a television camera crew. Although I was very tired by this time, I perked up as I passed the cameraman. Not looking where I was going, I smiled at him and nodded as I passed. I didn't notice a steep gradient down the side of an embankment that dropped suddenly on my left! Consequently, my chair and I fell *head over 'wheels'* down the bank, breaking a fence on my way and landing upside down in a thick clump of nettles three feet high. I suffered a badly cut leg and was stung all over. When the cameraman and his colleagues, together with other alarmed walkers, dashed to my aid, I was so embarrassed as well as having much dented pride, all I could think of to say to the cameraman to retain some form of dignity and composure was, 'Did you get that, or do you want me to do it again?' This brought

Wirral Coastal Walk.

ribald peels of laughter that somewhat restored my dignity! The only other price I was paying due to my efforts was the constant pain and occasional weeping from my amputation scar. However, I deemed this to be a small price which was well worth paying!

Soon after my wheelchair confinement, I found that not everyone was the epitome of kindness to those who suffered physical disability. I started to find that able-bodied people tended to assume inhabitants of wheelchairs were somewhat non-comprehensive, deaf or perhaps even partially brain dead! I found that whenever I was out and about with Marje or other friends, it would be her or them who they would speak to ask how I was; it was never *me* who was asked!

Filming Swasie's arrival at the finish of the Coastal Walk.

It would be, 'How is he today?' This tended to offend and upset Marje a great deal, not to mention me as well. If people did actually talk to me, for some reason they would shout. However, Marje being the lady that she was would never inflame or magnify the situation by reacting in case it upset me. Although it did upset me a great deal, I too tried to ignore such inconsiderate behaviour to give Marje the impression that I hadn't noticed their, possibly unintentional, lack of tact and decorum.

When people tried to offer me their assistance they were always very politely refused. The times when I had to deal with a hazard or obstruction, people would hang around and stare with morbid and embarrassing curiosity to see how I would cope. Such behaviour made me feel 'freakish' and eventually this did start to get to me. However, I did try to maintain an element of dignity and courtesy at all times; I had to because I was becoming quite well-known for my fundraising. My self discipline did wear a bit thin on such occasions though! I soon painfully and angrily realised that it really *is* true, there *is* such a thing as the infamous 'Does he take sugar?' syndrome!

I'm sure that I speak for all those in wheelchairs when I describe the attitude and behaviour of many able-bodied people. It is no doubt very true that the majority of people genuinely wish to help those who are physically handicapped, but many times, tact and understanding without a doubt take a back seat and leave a lot to be desired. I can assure readers that being spoken *about* and not *to*, is very humiliating, demeaning and extremely annoying. Even if those responsible for such lack of tact do so unintentionally, it certainly illustrates the lack of disability awareness that still prevails in society. Even those who are strong-willed and fiercely independent have feelings of frustration and despair, and this attitude does very little to alleviate the situation. Since day one of my wheelchair confinement I have felt deep frustration due to such an unpleasant scenario. I have always tried to conceal my emotions to all. However, many times I was caught by Marje when she unexpectedly entered the room and caught me sitting there despondently, with tears rolling down my cheeks. This could have been due to nothing more than me causing a scratch on a polished cabinet with the wheelchair, or tearing the fabric of a chair as I negotiated the obstacles of a room. Frustration manifests itself in many ways, many times, due entirely to something extremely simple or trivial. Such occasions can then bring about many varied reactions such as anger, deep depression, feelings of inadequacy and acute hopelessness. These feelings can even be, and often are, life threatening. On such occasions it does not take much to cause a deep drop in morale.

I personally found, and still do, that I continually put on an act to convey to all that I am coping with adversity and disablement very well, when in actual fact, the very opposite is often the case.

CHAPTER THREE

Beyond Normal Limits

Whilst I was pushing my chair along the paths and shoreline during the Wirral Coastal Walk, I was approached by a lady who informed me that she was a member of the 'Friends of Leasowe Lighthouse' and that her group had recently renovated the 150ft structure which was over two hundred years old. The lighthouse is in fact a well-known coastal landmark overlooking the Irish Sea at Wirral's Moreton shore.

Taking things for granted, the lady went on to tell me that it was a pity that I couldn't admire the beautiful panoramic view from the top of the structure now that the public were able to be admitted. 'Why can't I too admire the view you describe?' I asked indignantly. The lady was clearly embarrassed (as I had intended) as she stuttered and stammered to find an appeasing answer. I helped her by retorting, 'You mean I can't see such a view because I'm in a wheelchair?' The lady stuttered a reply in the affirmative and beat a hasty retreat. I decided there and then that by hook or by crook I *would* get to the top of that lighthouse, so that I too could see the same beautiful, panoramic view that she so adequately described!

As well as trying to come to terms with my predicament by my physical activity I was also starting to write enthusiastically. Since the premature demise of my police career, I was astounded to have completed my autobiography; entitled *Off the Cuff* published by Mr David Roberts of Avid Publications, which was a total success. Once this reached the shops, together with various reviews via the media, my notoriety began to spread further. This additional publicity enhanced my fundraising activities remarkably. Encouraged by this

Selection of Swasie's books.

book's success, I went on to write my second book, *If the Cap Fits*, again published by Avid Publications. This too received good reviews and, as per *Off the Cuff*, copies were distributed to shops throughout the UK. Due to the triumph of my books, I started to write columns for various magazines and papers. I will *always* be grateful to Dave Roberts of Avid Publications for having the faith which put me on the successful road of 'authorship' and eventual acceptance into the writers' elite: the prestigious Society of Authors!

As a result of my books another 'string to my fundraising bow' emerged. I was asked by a solicitor friend who was a member of the 'Rotary' if I would give an after dinner address with regard to my fundraising exploits on the theme of 'Overcoming Adversity'. Although this would be a new experience to me, I nevertheless accepted his invitation with enthusiasm. Consequently, I gave my first after dinner talk to a large 'black tie' gathering of members of the Rotary establishment at the extremely prestigious Leasowe Castle

Hotel in Wallasey. My unscripted talk went well and I was amazed to receive a cheque for £500 for an hour's rhetoric regarding the cause of my disability and how I was trying to overcome its aftermath of adversity. The cheque, in its entirety as per all donations, went to my charity fund. Although I was pleased with my address and its subsequent generous financial donation, I felt that I could improve on this by way of illustrating my various endeavours via pictures during my 'sermons'! I gave this new avenue a lot of thought as to how I could put myself about and raise money by such talks. Marje, although pleased and proud of my recent achievements, was concerned that I didn't overdo things and kept a beady eye on me and my ongoing efforts.

Not forgetting my determination to complete my ascent to the top of Leasowe Lighthouse, I approached the Wirral Rangers Department with my request. Although they too were very sceptical, I managed to convince them that I could get to the top of the lighthouse unaided. My forthcoming event was announced in the local press. They had been informed of my 'eccentric' intention, which was to raise funds for Clatterbridge Hospital Cancer Research. Due to their enthusiastic coverage prior to the event, a large crowd was in attendance when I arrived on the day. As I entered the lighthouse one of the rangers offered to take my chair and place it to one side during my attempt. To this day I don't know why I replied, 'Oh no, where I go, the chair goes!' I must have been in 'senior officer mode' to have uttered such a verbal gem in front of all present, including the press. I had now inadvertently committed myself; the 135-foot climb was to be *with* my 47lb wheelchair! To say that I struggled and fought my way up the narrow, metal spiral staircase receiving cuts, scratches and bruises, is a gross understatement. However, would you believe it? I actually did it, chair and all. I was photographed at the top, sweating profusely and bleeding from a few cuts and bruises, as I looked out to sea, admiring the 'beautiful, panoramic view' that the lady had said would evade me because I was in a wheelchair. The illustrated article covering the

135ft Leasowe Lighthouse.

most unusual lighthouse climb, wheelchair and all, duly appeared in the local press. My dedicated fundraising endeavours were now well and truly starting to arouse interest far and wide, which in turn raised the profile and increased the coffers of what was then the Clatterbridge Gene Appeal (now the Clatterbridge Research Trust).

After the success of this event a close friend sarcastically bantered and suggested a repeat performance up New Brighton lighthouse. This sits guarding the entrance to the River Mersey at New Brighton and can only be reached at low tide after first negotiating moss-covered rocks, rock pools, mud and sand. At the time I laughed the matter off, but giving this suggestion some further thought, I was quick to realise that such an 'impossible' ascent would be a *real* achievement. I decided to try and make my friend eat her words! I contacted the owner of the lighthouse, the late Mr Norman Kingham. At first he thought I was joking as he deemed it would first be virtually impossible to even *reach* the lighthouse in a wheelchair, let alone climb it. He then informed me that there was also the small matter of a moat around the structure which, even at low water, was at least two feet deep. Not willing to concede, I insisted that I could, and would, get to the top of his lighthouse, again *with* my faithful chariot. The extremely benevolent and kind Mr Kingham would not deny me my chance. In fact he guaranteed me a substantial donation if I succeeded in my 'crazy' venture, which he thought would be physically impossible. Again, the press did me proud, although they too were sceptical and deemed that this attempt could well be 'a bridge too far'! The interest generated was phenomenal. An article, together with my picture, gave my brief fundraising history and announced my forthcoming attempt to ascend, with my wheelchair, to the top of what was considered an inaccessible lighthouse across the Mersey mudflats.

The day of this latest fundraising attempt was a beautiful, warm and sunny day. The resort was packed with weekend trippers and, on my arrival, I was surrounded by a large number of children and their parents who no doubt all wondered if I could *really* do what had been announced in the papers. I must admit, I too was *more* than a little apprehensive and even my close friends who accompanied me on the day didn't think I would pull this one off! With great difficulty I pushed my chair across the wet, slippery, green moss-covered rocks and even fell out of my chair into a rock pool. Undeterred, I continued on, struggling, sometimes backwards, across the sand and through the mud. It seemed to take an age. The kids who accompanied me shouted encouragement as I struggled and sweated. Finally, caked in mud I eventually reached the moat surrounding the lighthouse. I had got this far, and there was no way I was going to give up my venture now.

New Brighton Lighthouse.

The late Mr Doug Darroch (who would eventually become the owner of the lighthouse) furnished a short extension ladder so that I could reach the ladder that was built into the structure. This was twelve feet above and beyond the line of sharp barnacles and mussels that adhered to the structure's base. With the ladder in place I ventured into the cold seawater of the moat. As Mr Kinham had prophesied, the water was indeed deep, and cold, and came up above my seat; I became an *instant* soprano! In no time I was soaked through to the skin. I grabbed the ladder with my right hand and pulled myself up. I lifted my chair with my left hand and climbed to the other built in ladder and carried on upwards until eventually, after

Fort and rockpools.

what seemed an eternity, I reached the open door of the lighthouse about 30 feet above the ground. It had been an enormous struggle, but I managed to get my chair up and into the doorway at last. Pausing to recover from my strenuous effort I then proceeded up the narrow, wooden staircase inside until eventually I reached the top.

As I scrambled outside to be photographed sitting in my chair on the rusty balcony, a cheer went up from those below who had witnessed the successful ascent. Although I had sustained a couple of deep cuts and some bruises, I was elated. This event received a lot of publicity and I received many donations from those present on the foreshore. True to his word, Mr Kingham gave a substantial donation to my charity.

I was now giving talks to various organisations, associations and clubs to add to my charity. These included local Women's Institutes, church guilds and the occasional Round Table. Someone then suggested I attempt the Great North Run as this, being an extremely prestigious event, would be sure to raise a lot of money. As no standard issue NHS wheelchair had *ever* successfully completed this event I decided to apply to take part to become the first! Again, as when I applied to take part in the Wirral Coastal Walk, the authorities explained that they didn't think it would be possible to complete in a standard, castered chair what was normally undergone in an 'athletic' wheelchair event by wheelchair participants. However, as with the Wirral Walk, the authorities courteously allowed my entry.

This time, my ongoing efforts were to take an *extremely* dramatic turn! Fate was about to turn as nasty as it could possibly be.

CHAPTER FOUR

Inconsolable Devastation

After my acceptance into the Great North Run I was grateful to receive sponsorship from the very kind Mr John Taylor, a director of Drayton Motors and one of the peninsula's main Volvo Agents and dealers in Bebington, Wirral. The very prestigious vehicle business is held in high esteem amongst the motoring fraternity as Drayton Motors is a family owned business and has served the area admirably for the past 27 years. To assist my Clatterbridge Cancer Charity fund, the extremely kind and caring Mr Taylor offered the loan of a new Volvo to take me and a film camera crew up to Newcastle to film my participation in the event. As this would be a 'first' for an ordinary wheelchair, I was to be subject of a subsequent documentary film to be produced by Mr Ali Boxie featuring my fundraising endeavours entitled 'The Millennium Man'. The documentary, made and filmed by 'Wirral Inroads' of Birkenhead, would highlight my fundraising charity endeavours to overcome adversity as well as hopefully being an entertaining incentive to those who are physically handicapped. This was an extremely generous offer and would provide transport for me, my son Ron and Marje also, as she expressed her desire to accompany me. Mr Taylor had even ensured that the vehicle's fuel tank would be full (at his expense) prior to our departure. This illustrates the standard of customer care which is the well established norm at Drayton Motors.

As the Great North Run event approached, I had booked Marje, my son Ron and myself into a hotel near the finishing line at Mowbry Road, South Shields. My camera crew too would be staying at the same venue. All appeared to be on course for my first major endeavour and I looked forward to it with extreme enthusiasm. However, as the event drew closer, Marje started to feel unwell. She had been encouraged to attend regular evening bingo sessions by her elder sister Elsie, an ardent bingo addict. The venue of these sessions was the old Birkenhead Plaza cinema. This was a very smoky environment and although Marje was reluctant to go to the sessions, nevertheless she conceded to her sister's insistence to accompany her each week. I am a vehement anti smoker and as Marje returned home from her first visit, I was appalled when I could smell the thick acrid smoke on her clothes and in her hair. On my mentioning this Marje admitted that she too detested those people smoking near her, especially one of her company who was an addicted chain smoker. I begged her not to go again but Marje's reluctance was always overcome by her sister's overbearing insistence as she was always emphasising when she rang, 'You'll *have* to come, I've bought the tickets now!' I became very annoyed, and eventually her sister and I fell out when I pointed out to her the lack of consideration shown to someone who should not be in a smoke-ridden environment. I was severely chastised by my wife for upsetting her sister!

Throughout our married life Marje's elder sister and I had *never* enjoyed an amicable relationship due to her continual interference. Now this latest scenario was to cause me a lot of anxiety and severe frustration as I couldn't stop the weekly forays down to that confounded bingo hall in Birkenhead, where Marje would return with her hair and clothes reeking of foul cigarette smoke. That was only on the outside, so what must have been going *inside*? Many times she would come home breathless and would constantly need the assistance of an inhaler. How I cursed that bloody bingo hall, its equally selfish and inconsiderate smokers *and* her domineering sister!

I continued my daily high mileage wheelchair pushes and Marje contentedly remained at her 'happy little job' as she called it. However, she started to feel unwell and couldn't shake this off. She started to suffer from breathlessness. She visited our GP who diagnosed this to be due to her asthma and increased the dosage of her inhaler. Eventually, as things showed no sign of improvement I was forced to call our doctor to her. I started to worry as Marje became more and more lethargic and just wanted to lie down. This was *totally* unlike her. Our GP referred her to a consultant and it was consequently revealed that she had 'a shadow' on her lung! Tests were carried out and X-rays taken. At first she was diagnosed with having pneumonia. She was treated and given medication, and due to her severe discomfort she reluctantly had to go off work sick. Marje's condition deteriorated and she was now becoming constantly out of breath.

The time came for me to travel north for the Great North Run. Marje by now was so ill that it was obvious she would not be able to accompany me. I decided that my place was with my wife and I would cancel my participation and stay at home with her. She wouldn't hear of this and emphatically insisted that I go ahead and complete the event. I wanted to take her with me, but as this was not possible I intended, on my completion of the 'run', to place my medal round the neck of my heroine, my Marje. Nothing would now stop me completing the arduous Great North Run in my castered 'tank'. I knew it would be hard but I was also determined that I would become the event's *first* standard NHS wheelchair to successfully complete the long and hilly course. Even the proverbial 'wild horses' would not prevent my forthcoming endeavour to be anything but successful. This was special; this would be just for Marje!

After a press interview at Drayton Motors, Ron, my camera crew, Mr Ali Boxie, his assistant Ruth together with Miss Jan Heyes (the then Cancer Gene Appeal co-ordinator at Clatterbridge Hospital) and me, were pictured alongside our shiny new Volvo car. Ironically the venue is exactly opposite the Cancer Research establishment at Clatterbridge Hospital. After press operations were concluded we set off for distant Newcastle where I would hopefully make wheelchair history the following day.

Although I was confident and happy at the privilege of taking part in such a high profile and elite event, I was however sad that Marje was not with me on such an important occasion. Never mind; this blight would be overcome when I returned and placed the medal round her neck. I was *really* looking forward to that.

Our trip up north was pleasant and uneventful. On arrival, as previously arranged, we were met by an off duty police motor cyclist friend Gary Waine, who guided us to our hotel. The hotel was near the event's finish on the sea front at South Shields. It was not exactly the best of venues. I had to insist that the lock to my room was repaired as it was totally insecure. The place was a little on the grubby side to say the least, but alas it would have to do. I would certainly have been more pedantic if Marje had been with us! As there were a few hours to spare I paid a visit to my old friend and ex-police colleague, Bill Cram and his lovely wife Mia, the parents of the well-known and infamous athlete Steve Cram. I spent a pleasant afternoon with them and their son and all three promised to see me en-route during the 'run' the following day. They also each gave me a substantial and generous donation to my charity.

Back at 'Grubby Castle' I prepared myself for the mega challenge of the forthcoming day. After an early supper I turned in for the night after telephoning my wife. My wonderful better half wished me well and told me that she looked forward to wearing 'her' medal on my return after the event. When I said goodbye I found that I couldn't get to sleep. I tossed and turned throughout the night, thinking of the big day that was to come. I rose at 6.00am rearing to go and was up, washed, dressed and ready for anything by 7.30am. After a hearty breakfast we left our dingy hotel and made for the start of the run.

On our arrival I was amazed at the sheer volume of people gathering at the line; there were literally thousands, all milling around waiting to take their place at the start. TV cameras, police, ambulances and officials were everywhere. The activity was phenomenal. The atmosphere was one of positive enthusiasm.

Start of the Great North Run.

Everyone was extremely friendly, and many were in fancy dress to colour and enliven their fundraising participation during the event.

I had the unique and proud privilege of being introduced to the masses via the event's public address system as being the first ever, standard, NHS wheelchair to attempt the Great North Run. I was truly amazed and humbled at the rapturous applause I received from the massive crowds as I set off. I was allowed to start my push ten minutes before the official start, to enable me to get clear of the mass of runners that would cascade down the highway at the firing of the starting gun. The event was very hard due to some of the long steep hills. Even downhill my speed could not go over three or four miles

Motorcycle cameraman filming Swasie during the Great North Run.

per hour; sometimes I even had to push *downhill!* The athletes' lightweight wheelchairs however, flew past me in no time. *Their* machines were capable of reaching speeds of up to 50mph plus! Very soon I was engulfed by a mass of runners. However, at no time was I a hindrance to anyone and I pushed on relentlessly. It was a very hot, sunny day and soon my gloveless hands were becoming sore due to them sweating, causing the skin to soften and blister. My endeavours and constant progress were pedantically filmed by my cameraman Ali Boxie from his lofty pinnacle of a film unit motorcycle driven by Traffic Cop Gary Waine. It was due entirely to Gary's organising efforts that the whole of our trip up north to the event would be a resounding success. I will remain forever grateful to him for organising our trip up in 'Geordie land'.

The long and hard slog eventually reached the steep, downhill slope onto the South Shields seafront at the finish. I had completed my first big sporting endeavour in three hours and five minutes! I proudly received the GNR medal but my euphoria was tinged with sadness at Marje's absence. However, I would soon be back home where I would place the medal where I considered it *truly* belonged and deserved to be. At the conclusion of celebrations and festivities at the end of the run, I jubilantly returned with my equally proud entourage back home to Wirral. My Great North Run venture would raise much-needed funds for the Clatterbridge Cancer Gene Appeal. This was ably assisted by the publicity my endeavour received via the media. Ali Boxie's film footage would be subsequently included into his film 'The Millennium Man'!

Back home my moment of sheer, deep pride came when, in front of Ron, Jo and a couple of close friends, I placed the Great North Run medal around Marje's neck and took a photograph of her with *her* prestigious medal. Although Marje looked very tired and drawn, she nevertheless wore it with pride. The image of her sitting there adorning the new medal brought a lump to my throat as it was obvious that my poor wife was now becoming *very* ill. Oh, how I wished she could have been well enough to have accompanied me up north for the great event.

As the days went by, I was now writing my third book, *Onto the Final Leg*. I was still continuing my daily wheelchair forays of ten to fifteen miles, and began giving talks to various schools, clubs and associations. *All* of these commitments were for the sole purpose of generating funds for my charity, and at the same time making sure that I looked after my beloved wife.

Marje's health started to cause more concern and I had to curb my activities. She was becoming breathless and more lethargic. She felt so bad that to my utter relief and delight, she finally refused her sister's dominant requests to attend that confounded bingo! She

Swasie's beloved Marje wearing her medal.

insisted that she only went to 'keep her sister happy and save any hassle', which was very typical of her. All she continually wanted to do was lie down. She sometimes didn't even want the company of me or our son and daughter. Things were really getting bad. Once again I summoned our GP. Our trusty doctor unhesitatingly attended and immediately referred Marje to a hospital specialist, Dr 'Dieslaf' (not his real name). On seeing him, he was concerned that the 'shadow' on Marje's lung could be more serious than had first been anticipated. Tests were carried out and they revealed that Marje's lungs were filling with fluid. She was fully examined and it was decided to admit her right away. Her pneumonia was raging; her lungs were so full she was almost drowning! When I left her to return home I was very upset and extremely distressed.

I returned to the hospital the following day and was relieved to find that Marje looked a lot better. A tube had been inserted into her back to drain the fluid from her lungs. I was told that she may be allowed home in a few days *if* her condition continued to improve and she responded to treatment. That was brilliant news.

Although I was at the hospital every minute I was allowed, I nevertheless felt very lonely and vulnerable during her absence. The shortcomings of my disability were brought home to me with a vengeance when I was alone at home. Even the simplest of chores to a 'normal' person were astronomical tasks to a solo wheelchair pilot. I realised just how awkward and difficult some tasks were. The whole scenario was very depressing and this was magnified alarmingly by my constant worry about the state of Marje's health. I started to panic and think the worst. What was in store for me? But, more importantly, what was in store for my poor suffering wife? The situation gave a chilling illustration as to how we *all* take things for granted when things are 'normal'. Being able-bodied and living with one's wife or husband, going to work and raising a family are all accepted as routine. However, when the wheel comes off and things are totally different, oh, how life can then rapidly deteriorate and plummet into a series of crises! How utterly unprepared we all are for the dramas and obstacles that suddenly manifest themselves and shatter our totally assumed way of life. During my operational police career I have many times attended 'domestic disputes' as they are officially termed. I have seen the results of these disputes and witnessed the unsavoury sight of battered and bleeding wives, who have received horrendous injuries from physically superior husbands, partners or boyfriends. In some cases the opposite was the case where females had assaulted males. I cannot tolerate men hitting, injuring and knocking females about. This behaviour is totally abhorrent and unacceptable, for whatever reason. I have never been able to understand why men could even consider violence as an option during even the most heated dispute with their other half!

Thoughts like this made me bitter and extremely angry. If only those who behaved violently towards their partners would realise just how lucky they were having a partner, wife or husband. Couples like this, I selfishly thought, were allowed to live 'healthily' ever after! Nothing *ever* happened to them! I would need to keep firm, to keep in control as I must ensure that I would be able, and capable, of looking after my wife during such crises as I was now experiencing. However, this would be easier said than done; I would need all the mental and physical power and strength that I could muster!

After five long days, the love of my life returned home to recover and hopefully get herself back to normal. I felt sheer relief and gratitude at having her back. I looked forward to her return to work as this would hopefully illustrate that once again, things were almost as good as they had been. Marje too was desperate to return to her 'happy little job' amongst her colleagues and customers, but there was no chance of that at the moment. I breathed a sigh of relief. Things appeared to be going well again.

Although at first Marje seemed to be okay, I was certain that I could detect something in her eyes that frightened me and told me that things just didn't seem right. I repeatedly asked her how she was but typically, she insisted all was well with her. Oh, how I was *so* thankful that I had fulfilled a lifelong promise to her just before my amputation. When my premature retirement was *forced* upon me I whisked her away on a Caribbean cruise at the first available opportunity. This was to say a big thank you to her for all the wonderful years she had given me during our happy marriage. It was also to try and compensate her for all the suffering she had endured throughout the many years when I had been injured or hospitalised. There were indeed many such times during my years in the emergency services; *too* many! The cruise was an extremely therapeutic and beneficial period for both of us. It had, without doubt, been the most efficient chill out we could have wished for. However, my apprehension continued, and I couldn't put my finger

Marje and Swasie on their cruise.

on what it was that was causing me so much concern. I sincerely hoped my depressing thoughts would prove to be totally unfounded, but I knew deep down that Marje was far from being 'out of the woods' regarding her health. I was frightened! I had a secret dread as to what the not too distant future might hold. For once in my life, I hoped to hell that my usual confident opinions were wrong.

I appeared on local radio, and started to experience what could almost be termed as 'celebrity' status on occasions! However, hand on heart, vanity did not come into the equation in *any* manner or form; I was just proud and privileged at having created such an impact in the field of fundraising. On the other hand, I was overjoyed that Marje was proud of my efforts but, being a rather shy and modest person, she sometimes found sitting at 'top' tables to be a little overbearing. I found doors that were previously inaccessible were starting to open. Marje and I were invited to various functions where I would be presented with donations of extremely generous amounts for Clatterbridge. This new development wasn't something I had expected; however, I was certainly proud of meeting various dignitaries and others from all walks of life and various professions. I was also pleasantly and inadvertently enhancing my circle of friends and, more importantly, the coffers of my fund.

Only a couple of weeks had passed before Marje started to feel unwell again. Together, we went to the hospital for her to be seen by a doctor. I was asked to call back later and on my return I was advised that it would be a week or so before we would know anything. I collected my wife and we returned home. How I prayed that all would be well with my suffering wife. As the result of Marje's latest hospital visit, the two of us were asked to see the specialist, Dr 'Dieslaf'. At the time and date appointed Marje and I went to the hospital with feelings of deep trepidation. I put on an act to indicate that all would be well and it would be just another routine visit to say all was going okay. However, deep down I was just as petrified as Marje, and dreaded what our visit would reveal. It wasn't long after our arrival that Marje and I were admitted in to the consulting room to see the specialist who had sent for us. As I wheeled myself in alongside Marje, I looked at the doctor's face for any indication that the forthcoming news might be positive. There was none. Although extremely courteous, as soon as the doctor spoke, his sombre and formal tone immediately conveyed to me that things were not going to be good.

This visit would end up being the worst time in my whole life. The news was unbearably shattering. My lovely wife now had lung cancer. To make matters worse, the cancer was terminal and at an advanced stage. Marje sat stone faced and tried, as usual for my sake, to minimise the serious, life threatening state of affairs that now confronted her. My mind was in turmoil; I too tried desperately to retain my self control. At the end of our consultation, I took Marje's hand in mine and propelled my chair with the other, leading her from the room. Once outside, Marje bent down and put her arms around me and, clinging desperately, said 'I'm so frightened, I love you so much, I don't want to die.' Her last comment stung me beyond words. Marje then sobbed, 'I'm worried for you, how the hell will you manage when I've gone?' This almost cracked me up. I squeezed her tight, hiding my face from her as the tears rolled uncontrollably down my heartbroken face. All I could say to her was, 'Hey! Don't you be talking like that. Doctors are not *always* right you know!' I went on to add that there are many cancers being treated successfully or even totally cured.

My latter remarks were futile to Marje and even to myself, but it was all I could do to try and help pacify my frightened and alarmed wife during the darkest period of her life. We both cuddled like a couple of infatuated teenagers at the back of a bike shed! I smothered Marje with kisses and hugs outside Clatterbridge Oncology department like there was no tomorrow. We were totally oblivious to the stares of others as they passed us by. Ron then arrived with his sister Jo to collect us. They came to pick us up from the hospital hoping to take us for a 'celebratory' meal once we had learned that all would be well. His well-intentioned gesture was

Swasie's son Ron.

sadly not to be. Ron knew right away that things were bad. However hard Marje and I tried to put on a brave face in front of our offspring, at least until we arrived home, Ron could see right through the pair of us.

'How did you get on Mum?' he asked quietly.

'Let's get in the car first where we can talk in comfort', I stalled quickly and tactfully to spare Marje having to reply. Once inside the car, Marje sat in the back with Jo and we set off to return home. Ron turned to me again.

'Well? C'mon dad, tell me.'

'I'll explain all when we get home, but things are not good I'm afraid son' I replied, as quietly as I could because I didn't want Jo to hear until I could decide how to break the news to her also. I tried to make divertive conversation as Marje sat in the back, no doubt terrified out of her mind.

'What did the doctor say mum?' I heard Jo ask.

Marje replied, 'Er, just that......er...just...'

I cut in to ease Marje's discomfort, 'I'll tell you all about things when we get back home Jo'.

'Is it *bad* mum?' persisted Jo.

'It's not good Jo, but I'll tell you when we get back. Mum's upset so leave it to me pet'. With that, we all remained silent for the rest of the journey. It seemed like hours before we reached our bungalow home, but in fact the journey had only taken twenty minutes. Once inside the confines of our home Marje excused herself, saying she was going to the bathroom. I asked Jo to make us all a cup of tea then propelled my chair along the hall to check if Marje was okay. She wasn't in the bathroom; she was sitting on the side of the bed, staring, wet-eyed, into space. I wheeled myself into the room. 'I don't want to leave you and the kids' she sobbed. I placed my arm around her and hugged her. 'You *won't* leave us' I reassured her, knowing damned well I was talking through my backside. 'Come in when you're ready sweetheart, Jo's just made us a cup of tea', I said as calmly as I could. I returned to the lounge and noted that Ron and Jo were sitting together on the settee awaiting my update regarding the hospital visit. I envisaged Ron would be stronger as he was a serving police officer, and hopefully his own experience of tragedy as well as his training would at least help him a little. Jo however, would perhaps not be able to take the news as I hoped she might! Although I tried to be as tactful as I could, I also had to be *totally* candid with them both. Thankfully they were at least both adults and would understand the gravity of the situation.

Marje remained absent from the room as I told our two 'children' exactly how things stood. As expected, Jo burst into tears and sobbed, 'But mum was getting on okay dad', as if pleading for me to put the clock back. To my surprise, a very subdued Ron looked me straight in the eye and cursed before saying slowly, 'You don't think the bloody smoke at the bingo had anything to do with this do you?' I looked at my son and didn't hesitate to tell him that in my opinion, my worst fears regarding his mother's attendance at that cursed bingo hall in Birkenhead had now been brought about.

'Seeing as you mention it Ron, now I'll tell you; yes I bloody *do* think *just* that', I growled bitterly. I told him that I had thought all along the outcome of his mother's attending at such an inhospitable, smoky environment such as the Plaza Bingo hall would bring about *exactly* what had happened. Nothing whatsoever would ever change my opinion on that!

I was well and truly aware of what had similarly happened to a much loved and well-known personality in the entertainment world. I have been a lifelong fan of the greatest versatile funny man ever: the well-known and equally well loved comedian, Roy Castle. He too had paid dearly for frequenting such an environment during his professional career as a top entertainer. It is to Roy's widow Fiona, herself a relentless fundraiser for Cancer Research and other worthy causes, that I am eternally grateful for the honour and privilege of her writing the foreword to this book. Fiona was awarded the OBE for services to charity, particularly to Global Care, an international Christian children's charity.

Swasie and his daughter Jo.

I have always *hated* smoking with a vengeance; both Marje and I were ardent non-smokers and since Marje's original diagnosis, I have been *more* than fully conscious of the risk and dangers of passive smoking. Oh, how I detest such a filthy, anti-social and dangerous habit. I equally detest those who so selfishly indulge in the offensive conduct when they are in the company of, or near to, sick people, particularly those who have respiratory difficulties, children and babies, those who are eating or those who simply do not wish to be contaminated with other people's residue. Annoyingly, such inconsiderate people just do *not* give a damn about those who are near them.

Suddenly, Jo couldn't contain herself any longer. She dashed out of the room and along to comfort her mum who was still sitting traumatised on the bed. I put my arm around the huge shoulders of my son and again, trying to hide my own tears, I whispered, 'We'll manage somehow Ron, we'll just *have* to stick together and *all* look after each other'! This again, was going to be a lot easier said than done.

My whole family was shattered and it was some time before we gathered ourselves together and decided what we were going to do about this, our most trying family crisis. We would have to unite in total strength and ensure that Marje would have our love, attention, support and assistance at all times. My anger would have to be put aside as it would affect the example I must set to Marje, Ron and Jo. Although I was absolutely devastated, I would do my best not to show it.

Irrespective of the fact that Marje was so ill, she made me promise her that I would carry on with my daily pushes, as she considered this to be therapeutic for me and wanted me to regain my fitness. She was also emphatic that I carry on at all costs with my Clatterbridge fundraising. I gave her my word; I would do as she asked and ensured that I did at least a ten-mile push each day. However, her welfare was my first priority and after my early morning 'outings' I would ensure that the rest of the day was spent fussing about at Marje's disposal. I was determined to make life as easy as possible for her. My son and daughter also ensured that their mum would want for nothing.

CHAPTER FIVE

Breaking of a Heart

Due to the deterioration of Marje's condition, it was now obvious that she would not be returning to work. Due to this and my own disability, I decided to take advantage of the mobility scheme and acquire a new car so that Marje and I could enjoy trips out into the countryside. This would also ease the burden of shopping and get my sick wife out and about instead of her just sitting at home. Having our own car would give us both a little independence and me some control over the transport situation as we had to rely on Ron to convey us to and from hospitals, visiting and shopping. During the time it took to complete the administration and formalities prior to obtaining delivery of the vehicle, sadly, Marje's condition continued to deteriorate.

As each day went on, Marje was not showing any signs of improvement. Early one morning Ron conveyed me, Jo and Marje off to hospital again. Marje had to attend the pathology lab at Clatterbridge for (yet more) blood tests. After this she was taken up to the wards to receive a copious amount of blood. Most of the day was spent waiting for Marje and eventually we were able to return to the comforts of our home. Marje's morale was very low; her depression and pessimism was heartbreaking. Ron, Jo and I tried to make encouraging conversation as we made our way home. Our efforts were to no avail as my wife sat totally morose staring out of the window at nothing in particular. However, things changed a little on our arrival back to the house. As Ron drew up at the gate, there, sitting proudly in the path was a shiny new car! I hadn't mentioned anything to Marje about us getting a new car and I had sworn Ron and Jo to secrecy as I wanted it to be a surprise. Although Marje wasn't feeling at all well, her eyes lit up and sparkled when I told her the car was ours and I would be taking her for days out. She managed a weak smile and grasped my hand. Giving me the added bonus of a kiss as she squeezed my hand she said, 'Thank you sweetheart, I look forward to that'. I intended to drive Marje to the ends of the earth and back to ensure she enjoyed her regular outings. Her appreciation of such a small gesture was most humbling. Her smile and comments completely made my day!

Two days later, although showing no signs of improvement, Marje insisted that we go out in the new car. This would be our first

Marje in the new car.

outing and Marje's face was a treat. I put my wheelchair into the back and off we set into the picturesque Wirral countryside. I drove to a well-known beauty spot at Thurstaston on the coast of the river Dee. There we sat, each admiring the view across to Wales as we savoured the refreshing delights of an iced lolly. I treasured this outing; I felt as though I was courting again as we sat like two teenagers romantically holding hands on the cliff top. Although the fresh air was obviously beneficial to Marje, she was however, still having difficulty with her breathing. I wanted our outing to last forever but sadly, after only a short time, we returned home so that Marje could go and lie down. We were only out for a couple of hours but at least we had 'christened' our new car for which I was exceedingly grateful. I hoped and prayed that these outings would continue for longer periods as time went on. Now that we had our little car I sincerely intended to 'make hay while the sun shone' as the saying goes.

Our little excursion must have taken it out on my poor, suffering wife because later that evening Marje felt quite sick. I rang our doctor who informed me that arrangements would be made for her to be admitted to hospital within the next couple of days. It looked as though our short 'honeymoon period' was over even before it had begun. The following morning I drove Marje to sit on the seafront at West Kirby. We were joined by Ron and his wife and the four of us went to a nearby café for coffee. However, Marje was feeling so unwell we had to leave and make for home. Once home I called the doctor. She duly attended and I was told to take Marje straight to nearby Arrowe Park hospital as her lungs had once again become congested. On arrival, Marje was seen and immediately admitted to a ward. There she was put to bed and a drain was inserted to release the fluid from her lungs. I was having difficulty accepting the situation and my concern was turning into abject fear at what the outcome might be. I could see that the strain was starting to show on the faces of Ron and Jo. The future held acute dread and I started to plummet into deep and severe depression. I tried desperately to keep a firm grip on my emotions as I could not bear the thought of life without my lifelong best pal, my rock, my *everything*. My dread caused me to lose my appetite and my nerves were starting to fray. I started to think 'naughty' thoughts about what I would do should anything happen to my beloved wife. These thoughts involved suicidal tendencies. If I lost Marje I just would *not* want to go on. My mind was in turmoil as I struggled to retain my self control. I must do this for the sake of Marje, Ron and Jo, I *must* stay firm, but how long could I keep up this charade?

Jo and I did our supermarket shopping between our regular and continual hospital visits. Marje's condition continued to deteriorate and one day prior to our hospital visit, Jo and I sat on the seafront as we waited for Ron to collect us. I sat at a local slipway and reminisced with a lump in my throat, as this was one of Marje's favourite specks. We would spend lengthy periods sitting eating fish and chips and feeding the ever hungry gulls. Here we would sit holding hands as we did in our courting days many years before. I have always been extremely sentimental and a sufferer of acute nostalgia, and although I was with Jo, the 'apple of my eye' I still longed for the company of my wife. How dearly I wished I could turn back the clock!

On our arrival at Marje's bedside, we were greeted with an upsetting sight. She now needed constant oxygen to assist her laboured breathing. The sight of her lying there with tubes and wires, dials and charts was heartbreaking. As always, I tried to hide how this was affecting me for the sake of Jo but this was difficult. Now matters were getting so serious that only immediate family were allowed to attend Marje's bedside. This caused rapid animosity and confrontation with Marje's sister. She adamantly accused *me* of deliberately 'engineering' this state of affairs to keep her away! Although this was absolutely and totally untrue, I was however, pleased that the presence of her overbearing, dominant and mischief-making sister had been curtailed. The hostility which ensued caused an irreparable rift between me and some of my friends due to the constant bandying about of false accusations and innuendos that emanated from a *very* bitter sister! My ongoing efforts to reassure her sister that I had nothing whatsoever to do with the visiting restrictions imposed, fell on completely deaf ears. She refused point blank to accept that they had been imposed *solely* by the hospital staff as Marje's condition was so critical. She then confronted the hospital staff, verbally abusing them and insisting she be allowed to attend Marje's bedside. Thankfully, the hospital would not budge one iota on the matter and visits were confined only to me, Jo and Ron. Unbeknown to me, Marje too had earlier *specifically instructed* this. The already distraught Jo was further upset by her father being verbally abused via her irate aunt's insulting telephone calls to our home. Thankfully, my wife never became aware of the distress her sister's conduct caused me and my children. This scenario continued for the whole period my poor beloved wife lay in hospital, which magnified the depression and deep upset my son, daughter and I were already experiencing. I pushed my chair to the hospital everyday and stayed for hours at a time. Even when Marje was dozing due to her sedating medication, I wouldn't move from her bed. I sat holding her hand whispering sweet nothings, hoping against hope that she would get over the severe state she was in. I prayed for her to improve; I refused to accept the inevitable outcome. I deliberately fought to keep such unbearable thoughts from my mind.

After a week had barely passed, I was summoned to Sister's office. There I was met by a grim faced Dr 'Dieslaf'. He sat down and, facing me, drew his chair close to my wheelchair. In a quiet, polite but sombre voice the specialist informed me that things were so bad that he considered that my wife had only a very short time to live. He informed me that they had fitted a 'driver' to Marje which would periodically pump diamorphine into her to ease the pain and sedate her. I sat there absolutely devastated. I had to think how the hell I was going to tell young Jo. It took ages before I could push myself from Sister's office back to Marje's bed. Although Marje appeared to be dozing she muttered something as I arrived back at her bed.

Jo said, 'Mum wants to tell you something dad'. I leaned over and placed my face near to Marje. She took my hand and spoke into my ear, 'You're a good man sweetheart. Thank you for being a good husband and father to Ronnie and Jo. I just want to tell you that I love you very, very much'. Now knowing what I did, I hugged my wife passionately and told her that I loved her too. I made an excuse to wheel myself to the nearby toilet, where, in solitude, I broke down uncontrollably. I just could *not* imagine life without my Marje. We had been together for well over 40 years. If she went, I would want to go also. If anything happened to my wife, I would not want to live. My head was full of unthinkable thoughts as to what would happen; how would I cope; how would Jo cope; how would Ron take the latest news? I would have to come clean to both of them as soon as possible. Although I had many, many times efficiently, professionally and successfully dealt with serious tragedies during my lengthy career in the emergency services, I could *not* come to terms with my own inconsolable situation.

Eventually, after what seemed like an age, I returned to my wife and daughter who had now been joined by Ron. A short time later, to make matters even worse, I was again summoned to see Sister. This time she informed me that Marje's sister had been on the phone again! Sister went on to tell me that she and her staff were now receiving repeated telephone calls abusing me and them, and insisting she be allowed to visit her sister. Her nastiness and verbal abuse only reinforced the decision of the medical staff. Had Marje been aware of this scenario there is no doubt it would have added considerably to her condition. I wholeheartedly supported the medical staff regarding their stance and now intended to make sure this arrangement would remain. I would certainly tell my two children about the added complication as well as the inconsolable news I had received from Dr 'Dieslaf'. I was now not only upset at my wife's condition, but also very annoyed at her sister's extremely vicious, audacious and outright wicked behaviour. For once, she could not get her own way even by her bullying and domineering attitude. I would be subject to her persevering onslaught for many more years to come!

My ongoing, regular visits to the ward never ceased. Ron, Jo and I ensured that Marje had at least one of us with her for most of the time. My daily visits to my wife's bedside were greeted with courtesy and sympathetic understanding by most of the sisters and nurses. Indeed the majority were extremely caring, and worked tirelessly to ensure their care was carried out to the letter. Without doubt they were the epitome of true and dedicated professionalism. Relatives and visitors were also in receipt of their compassion and attention. I will forever remain grateful to those sisters and nurses who certainly went out of their way to make sure Marje received nothing but the highest standards. Indeed, I too was *more* than adequately looked after by those 'angels' who manned the wards. I must also highlight those underestimated and normally forgotten cleaners and ward orderlies. The truly outstanding work carried out by those equally kind and dedicated ladies should be shouted from the rooftops. They performed their duties far beyond what was expected and required of them. I witnessed these wonderful ladies many times, unhesitatingly, assisting the nurses, fetching drinks, replenishing items, delivering and removing bedpans and many more unsavoury and (non-cleaning) jobs without the slightest hesitation. These ladies certainly are also unsung heroes of our hospitals' network.

Nevertheless, there were just one or two who were not of the calibre expected of members of their profession. I arrived at Marje's bedside one day to find Jo in a very distressed and exceedingly angry state. The cause of this was a young female doctor. As the doctor passed by my wife's bed she looked at her colleague and, giggling, wafted her hand in front of her nose and uttered an adverse comment about the 'vile stink' emanating from the patient she had passed, which happened to be Marje! She had inadvertently soiled herself as she was not now in control of her bodily functions. On hearing this I too was livid. I went straight to the ward Sister and complained bitterly. I underestimated the Sister's reaction. I thought she would 'close ranks' with her co-medic and promise to deal with the matter later. How wrong I was. The Sister was obviously a member of the 'old school' as she later summoned me back to her office. As I wheeled myself into Sister's 'inner sanctum' accompanied by my still distraught daughter, I saw that the offending doctor was also present and looking very sheepish! She appeared extremely nervous and was on the verge of tears. She had already been severely admonished by Sister and was instructed to offer an apology to my daughter and me. I was at this time, still extremely annoyed at the doctor's former lack of respect for my wife's dignity, as well as her additional lack of consideration and tact regarding my wife's serious condition. At first I could not be appeased. However, I couldn't help but admire the doctor's candour. She readily admitted to our allegations and went on to say that what she did was completely inexcusable and totally unprofessional. She offered us both her deep apologies. When she extended her hand for us to shake, I didn't refuse it as I felt that the Sister had dealt with the matter absolutely correctly and there the matter should now end. My daughter however, was not as forgiving, but she did, reluctantly, accept the doctor's apology. The doctor was clearly upset and no doubt fearful of a possible disciplinary outcome but to my knowledge the distasteful incident was killed off in the Sister's office. Neither Jo or I would ever forget that abhorrent and totally inexcusable faux pas, but the manner in which the incident was dealt with spoke volumes for Sister's professionalism and integrity.

As time went on I would sit at Marje's bedside for hours, not getting any response whatsoever to my whispering of sweet nothings, cuddles and gentle kisses. During these heartbreaking periods, I would hold her hand or stroke her hair. Sometimes I would lie on the bed alongside her as it was far more comfortable (and intimate) than leaning over whilst sitting in my wheelchair. Other times I would gently wash her face and comb her hair when she was aware of my presence. I loved to spoon feed her ice cream when she would delight me by uttering faint words of thanks; other times she could manage to whisper to me that she loved me so much. She would squeeze my hand when words couldn't be spoken. Most times I would just sit and stare at her as she dozed, her plastic mask misting up as it supplied her constant, hissing flow of oxygen.

This brought about a second distressing incident, which involved a Macmillan nurse who deemed herself to be elevated far above her colleagues. She almost considered herself to be on a par with doctors with regard to her knowledge and experience in dealing with cancer patients. I found her aloof and sometimes overbearing attitude quite disturbing, even sometimes distressing. This particular lady's presence at my wife's bedside did not enhance my feelings towards her due to her belligerent and bombastic attitude. She gave me the impression that she held junior nurses in contempt or even scorn. On one occasion she even *told* me that she knew better than some of Marje's doctors! Out of sheer respect and hopefully maintaining the demeanour of an 'officer and a gentleman', I refrained from putting her in her place, especially as she came to administer treatment to my beloved wife.

However, things were to change!

One particularly distressing day Marje was having difficulty with her breathing. She leaned to me as I sat alongside her bed. We were holding hands and I could see she was trying to talk to me. I gently lifted her oxygen mask and put my ear to her mouth. She could only talk in whispers, 'Keep hold of me and don't leave me will you?' She added, 'give me a kiss' then gently her weak fingers squeezed my hand. I obliged immediately and hugged her to me as I did so. Marje then drifted into further slumber. I replaced her mask and lowered her head back onto the pillow. I now moved onto the bed and lay alongside her with my arm around her shoulders. Occasionally her eyes flickered and she gave me a smile before drifting back to sleep. As we lay there, I continued to whisper gently into her ear. While I was doing this, in walked 'Miss Prim and Proper'. 'Hey! Don't be talking to her, let her sleep and get off the bed and back into your chair' she instructed coldly, and went on, 'she needs all the rest she can get without you disturbing her'. No way was I going to adhere to this totally obnoxious and inconsiderate request; I treasured every minute I could have with my beloved wife. However, probably due to the shock of the nurse's audacious and offensive request, I did as I was ordered on this occasion and sat while the nurse adjusted Marje's pillow and blankets before looking at her medical notes at the foot of the bed. Oh, how I resented that awful woman. I absolutely loathed her attitude. She was equally bossy and rude to other nurses. After five minutes or so the nurse decided to leave but not before further admonishing me for trying to wake my wife. Enough was enough! I followed her out of the ward and gave her the biggest dressing down she had probably ever experienced. 'How dare you tell me not to speak to my wife when every bloody, precious minute is vital to us both?' I went on to inform her of her 'holier than thou' pedigree and abrasive, unfeeling attitude. She was told in no uncertain terms to moderate her attitude towards me in future. 'Miss Prim and Proper' then about turned and stormed off muttering her rhetoric of disapproval at someone daring to chastise *her*! Never again did that particular nurse utter any detrimental comments to me.

At first my wife's condition had seemed okay, although she did need to constantly wear an oxygen mask to assist her breathing. She did not complain of pain and was talkative and responsive to conversation. Her official condition for the first seven or eight days was 'poorly but comfortable'. However, when the 'driver' was inserted into my wife's chest with diamorphine among other drugs, she became lethargic and started to sleep for most of the time. This made communication increasingly difficult and in turn distressed myself as well as my son and daughter as we were gradually being deprived of being able to talk to her. As the lengthy drifts into sleep increased, I noticed that the diamorphine in the syringe had been increased from 20mg, to 25mg then further to 30mg. I certainly would not have agreed or approved of the syringe at all while she was not complaining of pain. Of course I would wish her to be as comfortable as possible, but why was there not any discussion or advice offered to me or my wife when she was in a condition to appreciate the advantages, disadvantages and dangers of the drug? As time went on Marje was made more and more unaware of her surroundings. Gradually she started to slip further downhill into almost continual and total sleep. I questioned the increasing of the diamorphine dosage and was repeatedly told that there were no such increases. I wasn't stupid; there *were* and I damned well knew it! My concerned sentiments were not shared with the medical or nursing profession however, and this did *not* stop the dosage increases. I was only too aware of various press items regarding incidents where allegations of euthanasia were made by relatives of patients who had died after allegedly being 'discreetly' overdosed with diamorphine.★ This does go on unabated and unauthorised in the guise of treatment for the elimination of pain and discomfort. Such decisions are even taken at nurse level, and this was verified to me by a Cancer Specialist nurse!

I had an angry confrontation with Dr 'Dieslaf' about the matter. Although he continued to insist that there had not been significant increases in the diamorphine dosage, I would not be appeased. I did accept that the 'driver' assisted to eliminate Marje's pain but at the same time it was also shortening her remaining period of life. I was devastated yet extremely angry; I was between the devil and the deep blue sea on the issue. There was no way and, in my opinion, no justification of dosage increase that would pacify me. I was obviously becoming a pain to those who were trying to do their best in the worst scenario! The deep love of my childhood sweetheart over-rode all other sentiment, causing blindness to any logic I possibly should have had. Did my want for Marje to stay with me stop me from considering her pain elimination? Such selfishness was overridden by my vehement desire to prolong her life for as long as I could; I considered the 'driver' was my enemy who was thwarting this!

In my opinion, it is time the public were made fully aware of the true capability of administering such treatment which I strongly consider to be almost equal to a 'conspiracy of eradication'. I will always hold a deep anger and resentment over the uninformed treatment and its repercussions. The 'driver' may ease the patient's pain and suffering, but it also unequivocally hastens their death. I believe each patient and their next of kin should be made fully aware of what the morphine 'driver' does and ultimately brings about. Its full advantageous and disadvantageous capability should be pedantically explained – to the letter. My opinion on the treatment of terminally ill patients is undoubtedly controversial but this opinion will never change.

*Ironically some years later, namely Tuesday, 15th February 2000, yet another article concerning the administering of diamorphine appeared in a National daily newspaper which highlighted my own 'layman's concerns' in 1997. The article included a photograph of Dr Robert Dickson. Dr Dickson, an ex-Police Surgeon of Doncaster, had treated two patients who later died due to being injected with diamorphine. Concerned relatives of the two deceased complained at the premature demise of their loved ones. It was revealed that the doctor had given injections of diamorphine to them. The injections were administered to ease the chest pains of one patient and as treatment for a swollen knee to the other. Dr Dickson was rapped by a coroner over the deaths and was reprimanded in 1990 by the General Medical Council. The doctor accepted the treatment was 'inappropriate and unsafe' at the time but said he acted in good faith.

CHAPTER SIX

Deprived of my 'Matrimonial Enchantment'

I continued my relentless vigil at Marje's bedside as her condition deteriorated. The standard of dedicated care by the doctors, nurse and ward orderlies knew no bounds. My reluctance to vacate the ward for even a short time did not go unnoticed by the ward Sister who was able to move my wife to a side ward where there was more space for my wheelchair. I will be eternally grateful for such an extremely kind consideration from someone who had far more important things on her plate than worrying about the relative of one of her patients. However, Sister's kind gesture certainly did make life a lot easier for me to come and go without disturbing the ongoing, busy routine of the ward. This side ward had a convenient door to a toilet. Again, this made things easy for me when I needed the facility. There was another door from outside which also gave access to this toilet.

As well as Sister's compassionate consideration regarding my predicament, her consideration further excelled beyond the norm. Due to the seriousness of my wife's condition which was now extremely serious, Sister somehow 'found' a camp bed which she surreptitiously brought in and placed between Marje's bed and the outer wall. This meant that I could virtually 'take up residence' and stay with Marje. Many times I would wake during the night from my 'cat naps' to administer a few sips of water or wet the lips of my wife as she lay dying. When she wanted to be spoon fed ice cream or tended to, I could oblige. In a small way this assisted the busy nurses. Such a gesture was *totally* beyond what would normally be expected. This sort of treatment should be shouted about from the rooftops when people savage the NHS hospitals and staff. Sister's kind, considerate gesture would remain with me for the rest of my life. If this had not been afforded to me I am sure that someone else would have been in receipt of Sister's equal kindness. I must reiterate my feelings towards the ward orderlies and cleaners. They too, without any hesitation whatsoever, constantly performed duties well beyond their normal requirements. Many times I witnessed them interrupt their cleaning chores to serve meals, wash dishes, deliver (and remove when used) bedpans to patients. They even assisted nurses by helping with bed making and removing blankets. Without doubt, they too are the unsung heroes and heroines of our NHS network. Even though I had severe critique regarding some issues, I also held a permanent and deep gratitude for the efforts of a mainly dedicated and caring staff throughout the whole of the rank structure. One or two who fell short did not, and do not, eliminate this categorical fact. As well as my anger at some things, I was also totally and utterly impressed by the efforts and standard of care afforded to the patients that I witnessed during my heartbreaking period at hospital.

Smoking was vehemently and relentlessly prohibited in the hospital for obvious reasons. However, in the early hours of one morning I was woken by Marje coughing. Immediately I could smell the foul, obnoxious and offensive reek of cigarette smoke. Puzzled, I climbed into my chair and propelled it outside the room and into the corridor; nothing! All was quiet except for the snoring, grunting or farting of one or two patients, and of course, Marje's cough. However there was no mistake; someone somewhere was definitely smoking. I wheeled along to the toilet door adjacent to Marje's side ward. I opened it slowly and silently then wheeled myself in. The door to the toilet cubicle was ajar. I pushed it open and there, blatantly sitting on the toilet seat with the lid down was a man dressed in pyjamas and dressing gown. He had in fact walked the length of his ward (where there was a toilet) to sneak into the rarely used toilet adjacent to my dying wife's side room. I was absolutely livid. As he appeared to be a reasonably young and fit looking man,

I was tempted to grab the front of his dressing gown and rip him out of the toilet cubicle and fling him down the corridor. Although I didn't physically touch him, I did threaten him that I *would* do just that if he didn't get his inconsiderate arse out of there in ten seconds flat. He certainly did vacate the toilet – fast. Not content with that, I then proceeded to follow him back to his ward before going on to the ward Sister's office where I related the blatant and inconsiderate scenario to an astonished and very angry Sister. Although I was not present at the administering of any form of 'retribution', Sister left me in no doubt that the selfish piece of utter low life would be suitably chastised. As I had total faith in her, this appeased my otherwise intense anger and I returned to 'our' side room.

On my return I was surprised to find Marje lying there with tears rolling down her cheeks and under her oxygen mask. Ill as she was, unfortunately she had heard my abusive and threatening rhetoric to the scum in the toilet and this had upset her a lot. Being the lady she was, she totally disliked any form of confrontation and, knowing my pedigree (which sometimes included a 'short fuse'), she had been frightened in case I became physical. She was absolutely right, and I was wrong! I should have kept the decibels of my verbal tirade down to prevent her being aware of the incident. I was not only very upset that I had caused Marje further distress, but I was once again extremely angry that someone should have brought this about by his total and blatant lack of care for those who were suffering. I swore to myself that no-one would ever again, in my presence, be able to pull another stunt like that, which would place sick people in further jeopardy.

As the days and nights went on, Marje slowly but surely was succumbing to continual administering of the toxic (albeit pain eliminating) 'driver'. Her lengthy periods of sleep were now the norm and I was suffering severe frustration at not being able to talk to her. One evening, she faintly called my name and I moved closer to her. She feebly took hold of my hand then whispered into my ear, 'I *do* love you sweetheart' before sinking back into the oblivion of enforced slumber. These extremely valuable words were now becoming less and less frequent as my wife's life was surely ebbing away. Every now and again I would feel her pulse to ensure that she was still with us. It was absolutely bloody heartbreaking. I feared I would lose her during each night as she lay in the semi darkness, the only illumination being from a solitary light in the corridor. The sounds of the constant hiss of the oxygen and the regular click of the confounded 'driver' as it pumped yet more morphine into her, will stay with me forever. However as long as the sound of the hissing varied up and down, I knew that Marje was still breathing.

One morning, at my request, Ron arrived with Jo to collect me from the hospital. I needed him to drive me a couple of miles away to complete some important business. I asked him to drop me at a specific place and remain there until I returned. On arrival he retrieved my chair from the back of his car and I told him and Jo I would be as quick as I could, before pushing myself off to my meeting. I left them both sitting in the car and propelled myself along the road and round a corner out of their sight.

The situation regarding Marje had now become extremely grave. I had been tactfully informed by the ever considerate and caring Sister that my dear wife could not survive for much longer – days at the most. I was advised to prepare for the worst. I sat pondering as to what on earth I should do next. I needed help and wasn't sure what to do in the event of the inevitable, traumatic scenario that was about to descend upon me and my two children. The only thing I could think of was to go immediately to speak to the local vicar so I rang him from the hospital to ask for an urgent appointment. After a brief explanation as to why, the very sympathetic minister, the Reverend Reg Walton, Vicar of Christchurch at Moreton, Wirral, arranged to see me forthwith. I felt absolutely disgusted with myself and unforgivably treacherous to my dying wife, as well as Ron and Jo. Why? Because I was virtually on my way to arrange Marje's funeral and she hadn't died yet! To this very day, I still feel total and utter shame thinking I had performed such an act. However, I was so scared of what was about to hit me and worried at what my responsibilities were, the only thing I could think of was to talk to a Minister of religion. It's ironic; although I *am* a Christian believer, very rarely have I graced the hallowed confines of a church other than the occasional wedding or funeral. Therefore I wouldn't have described myself as a 'religious' person, but, when the chips are down and help and guidance are needed, the first person one needs, and seeks help from, is religion and its ministers. In hindsight, how selfishly hypocritical this seems.

On arrival at the church office, I was warmly greeted by the Vicar. As I wheeled myself into his office he offered me his hand and

Christchurch, Moreton, Wirral.

introduced himself. 'Good morning, my name is Reg. Now then, what can I do for you?' he asked politely. I struggled to outline the circumstances which had brought me to him. My voice trembled and cracked with emotion. Tears streamed down my face as I described the predicament I was in; I needed his assistance, help and guidance to get me through what was about to happen. Of all the incidents, fatal accidents, sudden deaths, murders and mayhem that I had dealt with professionally in the past, I was now totally naked and devoid of the capability and fortitude I badly needed.

Reg listened patiently and tentatively to my ongoing renderings, during which I became totally distressed, fearful and apprehensive about what was to come. As we discussed the forthcoming church service, funeral and burial I found it difficult to apprehend that this was actually happening to me; that I was about to lose my lifelong partner, companion, pal and beloved wife of 40 happy years. We were discussing the imminent departure from this world of the girl I had been in love with since we were fourteen years of age!

After what seemed an eternity, Reg's consoling 'ministering' brought about the restoration of my composure and he made us both a cup of hot, sweet tea. Unbelievably, I felt as though a tonne weight had been lifted from my shoulders. Reg went on to tell me he would keep in touch and offered me his undivided help and attention during the forthcoming couple of weeks. I was exceedingly grateful for having visited Reg, and felt as though I could now confront the horrific period that was about to confront me. I somehow felt that whatever happened now, Reg would be there to help me as well as my children. As I pushed my chair back to rendezvous with Ron and Jo at the car, I now felt a lot more confident and at ease. On reaching the car Ron asked, 'Where the hell have you been dad?' As he drove me back to the hospital I told him the truth as to the reasons for visiting the vicar. This brought home to them the gravity of the situation that now prevailed. Jo sobbed and Ron sat, too choked for words. The three of us returned to the hospital to continue our vigil as we sat silently alongside Marje. She was sleeping peacefully and, thankfully, the hissing of the oxygen was still varying up and down indicating that all was at least 'okay'! Things were highly emotional for the three of us. We all vied for position to sit and hold her hand or caress or stroke her hair. Suddenly and unbelievably, Marje's eyes opened and with great effort she reached out her arms indicating she wanted us closer to her. She tried to say something but her words didn't materialise. She did, however, manage a smile; a smile that was worth a King's ransom! This lifted our previously rock bottom emotions to the ceiling.

As we all sat there a nurse came and asked us if we needed anything. I asked for ice cream which was duly delivered. When this arrived, I gently and tenderly spoon-fed this to an amazingly enthusiastic Marje. I was overjoyed, but I also felt deeply guilty at having done what I had earlier.

When Ron and Jo left later, I sat and pensively wandered down memory lane. I couldn't find any bad times; there were only good and happy times. I affectionately meandered through our teenage courtship, then our teenage wedding. This was followed by our honeymoon in Exeter. I thought about the arrival of our two children. We never ceased to be grateful that we had been blessed with a healthy son and then, fifteen years later, a healthy daughter. We had a blissfully happy marriage and although married life was a struggle at first, we eventually were able to move from flats to our own house. Finally we moved into our present bungalow home. Astonishingly, our bungalow, during its construction many years before, was the venue where we used to enter and kiss and cuddle when the workmen had left the site. Oh, what wonderfully treasured and irreplaceable memories we had.

I sat there mesmerised, knowing full well that I was undoubtedly now witnessing my wife's demise. She was sinking fast. I knew in my heart of hearts that I wouldn't have her for much longer. Every single day would now be a bonus. Oh, how I prayed to God to allow me to keep her. I dreaded the thought of life without my rock, my pillar of strength as she had been on many occasions. Now, when I needed her most, she was about to leave me. It just didn't bear thinking about. I lay on the bed with my arm around her as the night progressed. Oh, how those nights dragged on. I dozed in fits of shallow sleep. I sat in my chair with both arms around Marje as this was more comfortable. Now and again I would dampen a cloth to wet her lips. I stroked her hair and kept telling her how I loved her so very much.

Eventually I dozed and then after what seemed only a few minutes but in actual fact it must have been a few hours, I was woken by the sound of the oxygen – but this time the tone was different. It was now a *continual* hissing. Bloody hell! Did this mean Marje was not breathing? I moved my arms and then checked her pulse. There was no trace of a heartbeat. The only sound was of the oxygen emanating from the edges of Marje's mask – and the clicking of that bloody 'driver'! How I hated that 'driver'! I couldn't *believe* she had gone. I kept checking her pulse. I checked it at her wrist, then her neck, then back to her wrist – nothing. After what seemed an eternity, I decided to go and find a nurse, reluctantly leaving my wife. The time was 7.30am, Sunday, 12th October, only ten months since my amputation, and now, my wife had been taken from me. I sincerely hoped I was wrong, but on returning with the nurse who then summoned a colleague, Marje was pronounced dead. I couldn't believe that I had lost the love of my whole life. I was totally distraught, devastated and extremely angry. What the hell had she ever done to deserve this? The only consolation I had (although I didn't realise it at the time), was that we were not only together to the end, but that Marje had actually died in my arms as we embraced during her last hours. I was and have remained ever since profusely grateful for this, but also totally and permanently inconsolable at her demise at the young age of 58 years.

I refused to move from her room, even after being requested to do so by the nurses. I remained while nurses Jane and Sue cleaned, changed and laid Marje out on the bed. After this, they both kindly left me alone with her for a while as I tried to come to terms with what had happened. Eventually Sister arrived and gently persuaded me to accompany her back to her office from where I could ring Ron and Jo to inform them of the loss of their mum. Sister kindly furnished me with a cup of tea as we completed the sad formalities while I awaited the arrival of my two kids.

Without doubt, that period of my life was the absolute worst I have ever endured. Even my horrific injuries in days gone by were totally paled into insignificance as I sat there numb, trying to come to terms with my devastating loss. My mind was in turmoil. I wanted Jo and Ron there but I also wanted to go with Marje. I didn't want to go on living without her, but I must *not* let these sentiments show. In hindsight, I was at my lowest ebb ever and nothing or no-one could console me. Unless anyone has been down the road of extremely deep and severe grief, I am sure there is no other comparative feeling of such severe isolation. However highly trained one is, and I consider myself to be in this category, *nothing* can compensate for the feeling of desolation and loneliness after the loss of a loved one. The subsequent arrival of Ron and Jo helped me a lot as I knew I *had* to 'resume control' and maintain my composure. This I did with extreme effort and difficulty, but the fact that I had to console *them* helped me considerably to regain a certain amount of acceptance of the situation. The three of us would now have to look after one another and ensure that each of us could carry on with life without my treasured wife and their irreplaceable mum.

CHAPTER SEVEN
Manifestation of an Obsessive Crusade

The period I endured before, during and after Marje's funeral was the most traumatic I have ever experienced, such a trauma that an indelible mental scar has remained with me ever since. The Reverend Reg Walton was a tower of strength to me, Ron and Jo. Absolutely nothing was too much trouble for him. His visits were a therapeutic comfort for each of us. As well as maintaining his visits, these were interspersed with telephone calls to see if he could do anything further to relieve our grief. We will all remain eternally grateful for the personal and devoted care we received from this kind and comforting man.

I found that the grief, plus my disability predicament, magnified greatly the depression I experienced. I had also been diagnosed with 'post traumatic stress syndrome' due to my previous injuries. Although I had my two grown up children at hand whenever I needed them, I am ashamed and embarrassed to admit, at this particular time, that they were to be no consolation whatsoever. I was also suffering from the added problem of self pity. My severe injuries, followed by my wheelchair confinement, then the fatal blow of losing my wife had reduced a once rock hard, highly professional police sergeant to an absolute bloody wimp! Nothing or nobody could relieve my deep, depressive self sympathy and self pity.

During Marje's illness an old family friend of ours, Christine Lucas, regularly enquired and visited us to see how Marje was getting along, offering any help that she could. After Marje's death, during the time that I was at absolute rock bottom, Chris 'joined forces' with Ron and Jo and either individually or together, tried to be in my company as often as possible. Being in such company certainly helped me a great deal. In view of the fact that I had previously been raising funds for the Clatterbridge Hospital cancer charity ('my' charity!), Chris, in collusion with Ron and Jo, tactfully encouraged me to take up these activities once again. Slowly but surely their tactics started to bear fruit and pay dividends. Due *entirely* to their persistent encouragement, I realised that lethargy and self pity were *not* the roads to be travelling along. Realising that there were many others who were far, far worse off than myself (although at that time I couldn't envisage *what* could be a worse scenario!) I decided to appease my intense anger at Marje's loss. I decided to continue my

Chris (Matron).

fundraising with a vengeance by raising as much money as I could to aid medical research, to help eradicate cancer. My endeavours, however eccentric or unusual, would be to vehemently assist that fight so that no person would *ever* have to go through the pain and agony of losing a loved one to that horrendous disease.

Since Marje's funeral, I started a routine that prevails to this day. Each and every day I go to sit at her grave, irrespective of the weather; I never miss one single day. Leaving the house in the early hours I propel my wheelchair, accompanied by my German Shepherd dog alongside me at the end of his 'tracking' lead, and together we travel the eight-mile return trip. Once there, I sit in solace as my dog obediently lies alongside me and I remain there for whatever time it takes until I decide to return home. Although my 'chariot' is just an ordinary 47lb standard NHS type wheelchair, I have added two cycle lamps to the front, a rear view mirror, a cycle milometer and six red cycle lamps on the rear. This is not only to comply with road traffic lighting regulations, but also for my own protection and safety as my early morning visits to the cemetery are nearly always in total darkness. My police colleagues were curious at first as to why there were lights in the cemetery at 3.00am, but on discovering what they were, and the reason for my nocturnal sorties the sympathetic officers left me in peace. They still pass through the cemetery when they know I am in there just to make sure I am okay. Somehow my GP found out about my early morning visits and was at first very concerned. She tried to dissuade me from my unorthodox and certainly eccentric endeavours however, I would not be persuaded to cease my extremely important visits to Marje. Indeed, there would be no way I would even be coerced into this. I found being out and about in the early hours very peaceful. As my dog is not of an 'over friendly' temperament towards other dogs it also meant our walks were unusually quiet and uninterrupted. At first there were one or two occasions when the Police control room received calls from late night revellers or early morning travellers who, on seeing a vest and shorts-clad man in a wheelchair, especially

The shrine at Marje's grave.

during inclement winter weather, enquired if a 'patient had escaped from a nursing home'!

On the other side of the coin it did have its advantages, especially for the police and some householders. As I always have my mobile phone with me, I have dialled 999 on numerous occasions when I have seen something untoward during my travels. One morning, my dog detected a youth acting suspiciously and on shining my torch I could see he was trying to gain access to a house. I threatened to let the dog loose if he ran. The youth was detained until apprehended on arrival of the police. On another occasion I alerted a householder to a fire that had been started in a bin, which had been placed alongside his caravan parked on his drive. Thankfully the man was able to successfully extinguish the burning material and I continued my 'pilgrimage'. One wet and windy morning I was able to assist a distressed young lady motorist who had broken down on the lonely country lanes in the pouring rain. She was devoid of means of communication so I used my mobile phone to summon relatives to come for her. I remained with her until the arrival of her father who gratefully collected her and took her home; the car was picked up later. In addition to this, I have also been able to inform the authorities (via the police) of various problems, such as a dislodged manhole cover due to a water main burst, a strong smell of gas and trees in the road after a gale.

I still find my nocturnal journeys to be very therapeutic and consoling. Not surprisingly my daily mileage ensures that I maintain a high standard of stamina and fitness as these attributes are essential if I am to continue my fundraising endeavours.

As time went on, due to the encouragement from Chris and the kids I started to become known in the area for my continual pushes to raise money for the Clatterbridge Cancer Gene Appeal, as it then was. Chris would accompany me whenever her work duties (as a store detective) would allow. From the outset, Chris always carried her camera with her and soon became an ardent 'David Bailey'. Her photographic prowess would later extremely enhance and maximise my fundraising efforts to an unbelievable degree.

Having already successfully pushed a non stop fifteen-mile trek, I started to think as to how I could generate maximum interest in my future endeavours. Being blessed with having strong arms and upper body strength due to my years involved with boxing, the gym and weightlifting, I decided to try and push my trusty chair for very long, non stop distances. My first fundraising endeavour after her loss was to seek permission for me and my chair to climb another lighthouse. I contacted Mr McAlister, the owner of a well-known North West costal landmark, namely Talacre Lighthouse, Prestatyn, on the tip of the Dee Estuary on the North Wales coast. Mr McAlister's family business also included ownership of the static caravan park holiday homes among the nearby sand dunes. Although astounded at first, the extremely kind and benevolent Mr McAlister senior, listened patiently to my unusual request and on learning of the reasons as to *why* I wanted to do this, he enthusiastically granted his permission without any hesitation. Arrangements were then made for the lighthouse wheelchair ascent to take place, and in no time the local press and radio became aware of the forthcoming event via the 'bush telegraph'!

When the day arrived, Chris, with her trusty camera, drove me and my chair the 48 miles to the well-known landmark at Talacre beach. I was now about to 'kick start' my life's totally dedicated crusade of fundraising, in memory of my beloved Marje. As Chris parked the car at the caravan site, we were greeted by the friendly Mr McAlister and his son. The two gentlemen then escorted Chris and me to their nearby office where we were offered tea and biscuits by the kindly duo. Mr McAlister senior then produced a cheque and informed us that during a bingo evening at the site's social club the night before, nearly £80 had been raised by the club's patrons for my lighthouse endeavour. Mr McAlister then added, 'I put the rest to it to make it a round sum'! What an extremely kind gesture I thought as I placed the cheque into the pocket of my shorts. As a matter of etiquette I obviously didn't look at the cheque to see how much it was for as I assumed he had rounded it off to £100. Mr McAlister offered to transport me and my wheelchair over the sand dunes to the lighthouse in his Landrover. Not realising just how 'wheelchair unfriendly' sand hills are, I politely declined his offer, insisting I push myself the 400 yards to the structure. My difficult journey was obviously extremely hard, but eventually I made it. The subsequent climb was successfully completed and Chris, along with the press photographed me sitting in my trusty chair on the narrow balcony at the top of the lighthouse. After returning to its base I was interviewed at length by the press and local radio. During the climb there were many people on the beach who witnessed the spectacle

Talacre Lighthouse, North Wales.

and kindly contributed generous donations. At the conclusion of the endeavour I thanked all who had kindly donated to such a worthy cause. Finally I gave a grateful wave to our generous hosts, the McAlisters. Believing we had received about £50 or so in donations, a delighted Chris and I set off on our return journey home. As she drove along, Chris reminded me of Mr McAlister's cheque which I had forgotten about. I retrieved this from my pocket and unfolded it. I was gobsmacked! The cheque was for one *thousand* pounds. Due to the large amount of publicity the climb generated, this sum was increased considerably by further donations. I was elated at such a good financial outcome to my first endeavour, which

I thought would never happen. I thank Chris and my two children for this.

I was now determined to devote the rest of my life to the raising of funds for cancer research and other equally just and worthy causes. As well as my physically exhaustive efforts being therapeutic in coping with my crippling grief, there was still one big 'fly in the ointment'. My intense depression remained as deep as ever and never left me. I was also suffering horrendous nightmares during my restless slumbers. Years before, I was involved in a high speed police chase with a stolen car. As the driver constantly and erratically tried to escape me, the stolen vehicle crashed into a tree and the teenage driver and his two young passengers were killed. I had flashbacks of this, as well as regular flashbacks of my own horrific incident which had brought about my wheelchair confinement. Added to this was the highly magnified image and loud audible clicking of that confounded diamorphine 'driver', which had undoubtedly assisted in bringing about the end of my beloved Marje's life. Overriding these disturbing encounters was the stark, vivid image of the man who was responsible for the 'driver', Dr 'Dieslaf'. I *hated* this man with a vengeance! My nightmares caused me to wake in a cold sweat with tears of insatiable grief and frustration streaming down my face. I would jump out of bed, don my vest and shorts and immediately push my chair, accompanied by my dog, to seek the therapeutic solace of the early morning, eight-mile wheelchair push to Marje.

The daily visits to Marje helped me considerably with regards to dealing with my predicament. The physical exertion of the push seemed to psychologically 'burn off' my disturbing problems as I consumed the miles. People suffering various forms of trauma deal with their crises in many ways. I could have taken my own life and followed her; I can't deny that I *had* thought of doing this on *more* than one occasion. Alternatively, I could have turned to drink, or even drugs but my way of dealing with my 'gremlins' was to push my heavy chair for long distances, always with a visit to Marje first. What people think of my way of coping does not bother me one jot. My constant pushing is my method of overcoming adversity. What I could *not* erase from my troubled mind however, was Dr 'Dieslaf' and that bloody morphine 'driver'. This caused me ongoing anger. As explained, the malice I bore that particular doctor knew no bounds. Until this horrible scenario could be combated or eliminated, my bitterness would continue unabated.

Due to this, I constantly visited, and was monitored by, my wonderful and extremely helpful GP, Dr Marion Smethurst. Dr Smethurst treated, counselled and continually anointed me with her unique and tender balm of human kindness. She went to great lengths to ensure she remained in touch with me to safeguard my welfare. Dr Smethurst is, and will always remain, my true heroine. I consider her continual efforts to be well and truly beyond her duty and hold her in deep admiration and affection.

Being aware of my feelings regarding the 'driver' and Dr 'Dieslaf', Dr Smethurst decided to arrange for me to meet the consultant personally. She and I considered this would be the *only* way that I could attempt to sort these matters out with him once and for all. Despite the irregularity of a meeting between a specialist doctor and a 'layman' to discuss treatment of a patient, she would not let up in her attempts, as this matter was continually ripping me apart. Dr Smethurst firmly believed that only by Dr 'Dieslaf' having the courtesy and candour to discuss my problems, in private, would there be any chance of bringing my problem to a successful, or at least, amicable conclusion. On this she would not be moved and never once relented.

At long last, Dr 'Dieslaf' condescended to see me at his hospital consulting room. He promised my GP that he would candidly discuss the matter. At last I had the chance to question him regarding his use of the 'driver' and its dosage increases. I could also voice my critical sentiments regarding other things that had troubled me during my wife's stay in hospital. I was now to have the chance to eliminate what was an extremely painful and constant thorn in my side.

CHAPTER EIGHT

Killing some of the Gremlins

On arriving at his door I entered and was greeted by a nurse who said, 'Ah, Mr Turner, do come in, the doctor is expecting you'. She then disappeared saying she would go and inform Dr 'Dieslaf' that I had arrived. I sat in front of his large desk as I waited. He then emerged looking resplendent in his immaculately clean, starched white coat. The doctor extended his hand and said politely, 'Good morning Mr Turner, now, what can I do to help you?' I accepted his hand and shook it courteously. 'I think you know why I'm here doctor' I answered in a somewhat cool tone. I then proceeded to elaborate in lengthy and candid rhetoric to outline *exactly* what had been raging inside me since Marje's earlier hospital confinement. Dr 'Dieslaf' listened intently to my ongoing critique of both him and some of his colleagues. Not once did he interject or try to rebuff any of my strong allegations which were becoming quite emotive as I went on.

Throughout the whole of my 'acid' renditions, the doctor was the epitome of good manners and courtesy. I laboured on about the 'driver', the increasing of morphine dosage, the insensitive and curt conduct of a particular Macmillan nurse and even included the incident of the smoker. I didn't pull any punches whatsoever as I blamed a lot on the doctor personally. I elaborated as to how he had originally made a 'mis' diagnosis when Marje's lungs were filled to capacity with fluid, yet he let her return home. Due to this she then had to urgently return to hospital for further treatment as her health had rapidly deteriorated. The doctor was obviously taking into account my emotive state as he analysed everything I had to throw at him. Looking back, I don't doubt now, that most of what I was getting off my troubled chest may have been biased innuendo, brought about by blind anger and lack of interpretation. However, a lot of my critique was, I still consider, legitimate and fair.

Eventually my ramblings came to an end. I concluded by bitterly questioning why, after being in remission, Marje's condition became so fatal so quickly.

At the conclusion of my outpouring, I sat there feeling utterly drained; the tears of frustration and self pity rolled down my cheeks. During the whole and lengthy time I was firing my ammunition, not *once* did the doctor try to exonerate himself and his standards of professional care. I now started to look at him in a different light! The total contempt and bias conduct that I had held right up to my meeting with him, now started to evaporate. Having listened to everything I had to say, he once again offered me his hand and said, 'Okay, I'm sorry, sometimes I get it wrong'. I will never, ever forget those words of sheer candour. This forthright statement, from a person who could well have dismissed such a rhetorical onslaught, and from a layman at that, indicated what a *totally* honest man he is. I will always be the very first to admit without any hesitation whatsoever, that it took every bit of wind out of my sails. Who could fail to be impressed and appeased by such extreme sincerity? What volumes it said for the man's integrity.

Now it was his turn to speak and put the record straight. He went on to agree that some of my points were indeed salient, and that he would certainly 'take some of them on board' and bear them in mind in the future. He went to great lengths explaining about the difficulties of diagnosis and treatment regarding those who are struck with the many different forms of cancer. During all this time he spoke in educational volumes and remained nothing less than a thorough gentleman. I was certainly well and truly educated that day. He then went to equally great lengths to emphasise that the members of the medical profession are not super human and they, as others in many walks of life, don't always get it right. I unhesitatingly conceded this and accepted his point. I realised then how 'out of order' and even 'over the top' I must have been in my sometimes 'tunnel versioned' interpretation of what had been going on at the hospital. It was also explained that my wife's regular attending of the bingo sessions, in such a smoke-logged environment had, in his opinion, brought about an extremely aggressive and virulent form of lung cancer, which consequently and rapidly was to take her life. He was adamant that the bingo hall had certainly been a large, fatal contribution. We concluded our meeting, which unquestionably had turned out to be an enhancing and therapeutic 'consultation' for me. This time, as I left the doctor, I shook *his* hand vigorously and

Dr Smethurst.

enthusiastically and thanked him for his time. I fully admire and respect Dr 'Dieslaf' and appreciate what he did, or tried to do, for my wife.

Now that this major obstacle to my morale and continual well-being had been eliminated and the pressure had been released from my 'angry' chest, I could try and pick up the pieces and move on. Dr 'Dieslaf' had, in fact, killed most of my disruptive and troublesome gremlins. I will never forget that this was all brought about by the tireless and continued efforts of my fantastic GP, Dr Marion Smethurst.

CHAPTER NINE

Resuming in Earnest

The next major emotional hurdle I now had to negotiate, only six short weeks after losing Marje, was Christmas. I found this extremely hard to get through. As we had been such a close family, the festive season was always very special and we all looked forward to it with great enthusiasm. Marje and I always enjoyed Christmas, especially when the children were youngsters. Even now they were both grown up we were still as bad as young kids at this time. Although it is always an expensive time, this never stopped us both enjoying the festivities and the giving and receiving of presents. There was always the visiting of neighbours and relatives and the whole period was wonderful. Christmas Eve was spent preparing the turkey, last minute labelling and wrapping of presents and all the other equally enjoyable but busy things that ensured a happy Christmas period. This time however, I found things to be totally different. It was in fact heartbreaking.

I did try to ensure as best I could that the period would not be one of morose misery throughout the duration. As usual, my daughter Jo was busy fussing about, making sure that we did at least have some form of a Christmas. Sadly, however, I could not endure having decorations, a Christmas tree or boxes of crackers to pull. Even a turkey was conspicuous by its absence. There was no way I felt like entering into the spirit of festivity at all. On that first Christmas morning I was up and out onto the road at 3.00am to go and sit with Marje. Although it was very windy, the severe gales that had prevailed for the previous few days were thankfully starting to subside. Things were reasonably quiet as I made my return journey home at 5.30am.

I did see one or two revellers staggering home from a party or two the night before and I saw the lights go on in numerous houses as I passed. No doubt excited children were now opening Santa's overnight deliveries before they went to show off their new toys to their parents. It didn't seem five minutes since Marje and I were similarly subjected to my son Ron's enthusiastic renditions on the tin drum at five in the morning orJo waking us up with whatever doll or teddy bears she had received. I pensively reminisced as I pushed along, enviously looking up at those prematurely illuminated bedroom windows. Oh, how I missed those treasured, beautiful and wonderful times of days gone by. How I envied everyone who had a full family at this time. When I arrived back home Jo was up and awaiting my arrival with a hug, kiss and, 'Merry Christmas Dad', adding, 'I know it's not but you know what I mean!'

Having negotiated the Christmas and New Year festive period (with extreme difficulty) I pressed on with determination to ensure my fundraising continued and stayed 'on course'. I wondered exactly what my future now held for me. Little did I imagine, even in my wildest dreams, just how many guises these future endeavours would take or the extremes to which I would go to ensure they were successful.

I was constantly thinking of things to do that would be sure to generate a lot of interest, ensure maximum publicity and most importantly, increase the donations in my charity bucket. I still found that people tended to talk to those who were with me and not *to me*. They would audaciously and offensively ask Chris when she was out walking alongside me, 'How is he today?' or 'isn't he cold wearing just a vest and shorts in this weather?' I found this to be very annoying and because of this, I sarcastically started to refer to Chris as 'Matron'. Consequently, from then on she became fondly and affectionately known to everyone as my minder and mentor, the Matron! She would become my most ardent, capable and enthusiastic assistant in my constant quest to raise funds for worthy causes, whatever they may be.

Requests for me to give my talks continued to fill my 'After Dinner' engagements diary. As Matron had been pedantically recording my pushes and climbs on film I thought it would be a good idea if I were to illustrate any future talks with her pictures. The standard of the pictures was exemplary and when I gave my new 'illustrated' talks, they enhanced them to such a degree that the audience almost felt included in my endeavours! I was asked to talk to church guilds, Women's Institutes, Round Table, and many other private functions. Although slow at first, my list of 'clients' eventually started to grow rapidly. I found that I was becoming increasingly busy with my now *varied* methods of generating funds.

My fundraising activities are still mainly at my own personal expense. The cost of having Matron's pictures printed on large sheets was thankfully a lot cheaper than normal due to the generosity of the printer, once he became aware of what the pictures were to be used for. As time went on I had to get my pictures laminated as they were becoming grubby and crumpled with the regular handling. This was expensive due to the large number of pictures involved. Obviously the talks needed to be illustrated because of their unusual and somewhat unbelievable nature. I decided to find a new and more economical way of delivering the talks; the *only* way to do this, would be to invest in a portable projector. I shopped around and was astounded at the amount that these facilities cost. One company that continually gave to my cancer charity was a firm of office suppliers; Penkeths at Bromborough, Wirral. I decided to ask if they could help me with the cost of this new idea. I went along to speak to one of the firm's directors Mr Andrew Penketh who listened sympathetically to what I had to say. Together, we looked through his firm's catalogue. The overhead projector that suited my needs would cost the astronomical price of £680. I was gobsmacked! I never realised that such items were so expensive. However, there was no going back; if I was to continue including 'After Dinner' talks in my fundraising programme, I would *have* to move on from the 'antique' method I was presently using. Mr Penketh very kindly let me have a top of the

Swasie giving his first after dinner talk.

range, lightweight and powerful overhead projector for the extremely generous sum of £500. Although I was exceedingly grateful for such benevolent generosity, in all honesty, it was a price I could ill afford. Promising I would be back in a few days, I went home to ponder my next move. There really was no alternative. My obsessive intent to carry on with my fundraising meant I *had* to get the projector and I returned to Penkeths to take advantage of Andrew's generous offer. Thus armed with my new means to communicate my ongoing story of 'Overcoming Adversity' I then had to transfer all my existing pictures onto transparencies. This again would not be cheap. The well known phrase 'In for a penny,

In for a pound' now applied. I ensured that every picture I had been successfully demonstrating so far, would now be placed onto plastic transparencies before my next speaking engagement.

As Matron is from the Chester area, she suggested I push my chair along the walls which surround the ancient Roman city of Chester. Although not a long distance, I realised that this could well be a viable proposition as Chester is inundated with tourists, especially during the summer months. I decided to contact the Chester Tourist Board and inform them of my intention. I fixed a date and contacted the Cheshire Fire Brigade (my old brigade) and the local police. Cheshire Police headquarters were at that time situated near the Roman wall so I sought permission to start from the foyer of the building where we could have a press photo shoot. Everyone concerned excelled with their generous cooperation to ensure the event was a resounding success. The then Chief Constable of Cheshire Constabulary, Mr Nigel Burgess, kindly allowed the small gathering of myself, two of his beat officers, two Cheshire County Fire Brigade fire officers and an employee of the Chester Tourist Board, resplendent in his garb of a Roman Centurion, to pose for a press and PR photo shoot at the entrance to his H.Q. building. The sight of my ex-fire and police colleagues, and the Roman soldier immediately generated enormous interest. During the photo shoot most of those present donated generously to my bucket. The benevolent Mr Burgess appeared and he too gave a substantial donation. The three-mile push went well even though there was a downpour halfway round. I was accompanied throughout by the two police officers and the 'Centurion'; the firefighters had returned to their fire engine and made back to their station when we set off. The tourists, wishing to photograph the fascinating form of a Roman soldier on the Roman walls, willingly gave to my bucket on learning the reason for his presence. As well as being a total fundraising success, the event was also a resounding PR exercise for the police, the fire service and Chester Tourist Board. On completion of the walk we all returned to the Cheshire Police Headquarters canteen for welcome tea and refreshments, courtesy of the constabulary. Most of the officers, canteen staff and civilian personnel present, donated substantial amounts of cash into my bucket. The subsequent publicity, via features in the *Chester Chronicle*, *Chester Standard* and *Chester Evening Leader* all added to the benevolence as people became aware of the event that had taken place. This increased the Clatterbridge Hospital's Cancer Research fund considerably. It also shows the high esteem with which those members of the police and fire services are held by the general public.

From the very outset since the traumatic and irreplaceable loss of my wife, my daughter Jo, far from being conspicuous by her absence

Swasie with his escort, Walls of Chester.

during my pushes and climbs, has *never* ceased to keep in touch or keep her beady eye on me. When my endeavours take me away from home, Jo meticulously and efficiently keeps a constant vigil on the family 'squat' with her constant domestic chores. She ensures the dogs are fed and exercised and generally keeps everywhere 'shipshape'. Her undying and devoted care has *never* diminished one iota. She is without doubt the absolute 'apple of her dad's eye'! She and Matron never cease to ensure continual inspiration for my crusading efforts, in memory of my beloved Marje.

After thinking long and hard as to what my next challenging fundraiser would be, I decided on a *very* long distance wheelchair push that would hopefully raise a few eyebrows – and a few bob! Once again I contacted the McAlisters at Prestatyn. This time I asked if they would allow me to set off from their Talacre caravan site to push the 48 miles back to my home in Wirral. Mr McAlister sighed in disbelief but, again, he unhesitatingly gave his blessing to my cause and told me that his family would be more than pleased to grant my request. Consequently the benevolent McAlisters hosted Matron and me, as well as a documentary TV cameraman Mr Ali Boxie, who was to film the marathon push. Before our departure we were again treated to tea, scones and biscuits before I set off on my physically demanding non-stop journey of nearly 50 miles. Our little gathering was then graced with the arrival of two police officers in their traffic patrol car. The officers, who as always did not want to miss an opportunity, promptly joined us for a cuppa. I had previously and courteously informed the authorities of my road journey so that they were aware of a slow moving 'vehicle' travelling along the roads through their area. The police would put in an appearance somewhere along the line to check that all went smoothly and to ensure that safety was paramount. I must emphasise (to eliminate the possible wrath of ratepayers) that on such occasions, the police presence was *not* as an 'escort'. They were only there to *monitor* my progress via their normal, routine patrols. As we were about to leave, Mr McAlister handed me an envelope containing a cheque. 'This

Mr McAlister (Jnr) presents a very generous cheque.

is something from my family for your extremely worthy cause' he said before adding, 'we too, have experienced the trauma that cancer brings about'. I shook Mr McAlister's hand vigorously and thanked him for his, yet again, extremely kind benevolence, then bade everyone goodbye.

I followed my police 'colleagues' until they saw me safely onto the North Wales coastal road. They then resumed their patrol, occasionally returning to check my progress as I meandered along, burning up the miles under my wheels and casters. As with my previous lighthouse climb, the press and local radio were aware of my present lengthy trek. Whilst I was busy negotiating the highways and byways, I pulled the envelope Mr McAlister had given to me earlier from my pocket. I opened it and couldn't believe the amount that the cheque was for! Once again the McAlisters' generosity had excelled. They had given me a donation of £1,000. How kind and caring some people are. Such enthusiastic donating to my cause took my breath away.

Although none of my fundraising activities were, or would ever be, in any way intended as a 'vanity' exercise, I did purposely intend that everything I did was a wheelchair 'first'! Hence it was my intention to push and climb what many consider impossible. My thinking was that the successful completion of such things would bring about the donations I so eagerly sought for my charity. I will throw my hands up and readily admit that from the very start there certainly was, as the saying goes, 'method in my madness'!

I quickly realised just how advantageous it was to have the press and media reporting my efforts. I was pleasantly surprised when, due to this event being mentioned on the radio and in the local papers, people along my lengthy route came out of shops and houses to congratulate me on my efforts and donate generously. Even a farmer driving his tractor in a field shouted me to stop, just to give me a ten-pound note!

One amusing spectacle occurred as I passed through a busy little town towards the bridge which would take me across the river Dee

Swasie on his 41-mile non-stop push.

into England. Two ladies were putting some loose change into my bucket when a man, slightly the worse for drink, having consumed copious amounts of 'Liffy water' (Guinness), staggered out of a nearby pub and along to me. In a slurred voice, the inebriated man said loudly in his heavy Welsh accent, 'Here, take thish money – hic! I heard about you on the wireless this morning – isnit!' He proceeded to throw some money, wrapped in a five-pound note, into my bucket. I thanked him and resumed my journey. However, as I pushed away from him he suddenly shouted for me to stop. He again staggered to me and, slapping his trouser pockets with his hands, he audaciously asked, 'Hey, you 'aven't got the price of a pint 'ave you?' I resumed my journey giggling to myself at his cheek on becoming aware of his financial faux paux.

My first, (very) long distance wheelchair push had been a resounding success. I wrote a lengthy letter of gratitude to Mr McAlister as well as to the Chief Constables of the three police areas I had travelled through; namely North Wales, Cheshire and Merseyside. The ever faithful and highly efficient 'David Bailey' (aka Matron) ensured that my picture library was enhanced considerably for future inclusion into my illustrated talks. Eventually, the documentary footage filmed by Mr Ali Boxie would also be used. My fundraising capabilities were now becoming wide and varied. I was beginning to feel that my efforts of fundraising 'retribution' were starting to bite and I was now 'getting my own back' on that ruthless killer, Cancer!

CHAPTER TEN

Extending the Boundaries and Borders

As awareness of my fundraising exploits grew I was being regularly asked by other charities if I would help raise funds for their individual causes. There are many, many charities that are equally worthy and important causes as well as my own cancer appeal. However, I would be prepared to assist other charities, providing my own busy schedule would permit. My fundraising programme now included giving inspirational and motivating talks to schools, colleges, cottage hospitals and nursing homes. I found that I had to keep a stringent eye on my engagements diary to ensure that my numerous activities didn't over-ride each other. I couldn't bear the thought of letting anyone down by not being able to fulfil a promised engagement. Matron too kept a tight rein to make sure I didn't over stretch myself during what was becoming an increasingly busy and punishing regime.

Having successfully written two books, I now had the added honour and privilege of becoming the resident columnist in a very prestigious, glossy country magazine, the *Wirral Champion*. My columns no doubt upset some members of the 'establishment' now and again and my editor, the magazine's proprietor Mr John Birtwistle, soon described me as an 'editorial challenge'! I burned a lot of midnight oil maintaining my column but as I like writing, I felt this to be somewhat of a release valve which eased the pressures of my heavy fundraising schedule. During my fire and police service I was never one to keep my 'gob' shut when I deemed it necessary to voice an opinion to those members of the 'Chairbourne Infantry', sitting upstairs in their ivory towers along the corridors of power.

Many times I was summoned to the Chief Super's office to make his carpet more threadbare due to some misdemeanour caused by my dissent at something or other. I have never been one to hesitate in voicing my sentiments when I thought some particular form of critique should be brought to the notice, and for the benefit of, 'Joe public'. On the other hand, I never hesitated to afford glittering accolades or give maximum publicity to those who I deemed worthy or who I considered to be an asset to a sometimes selfish and inconsiderate society.

I didn't realise at first, but my 'controversial' columns were generating a lot of interest and support from the wide readership of *Champion* (either in vociferous agreement or the candescent opposite) and I was surprised that I was also acquiring somewhat of a 'following'. This was great! People would stop me to congratulate, criticise or discuss what they had recently read, or they would thank me for acknowledging something good that somebody had done. Many tended to give a generous donation to my Clatterbridge Cancer Fund as we conversed at the roadside or in the supermarket. I was now certainly adding *many* more strings to my already healthy and financially strong fundraising 'bow'.

To bring about my next challenging long distance endeavour, I set my sights on pushing the *whole* outer circuit of 'Ynys Mon'! I would propel my 'iron steed' around the lengthy and hilly coastline of the beautiful island of Anglesey, nestling in the choppy waters of the Irish Sea adjacent to the North Wales coastline. I was fully aware that this would be a *very* difficult and demanding task as there would be extremely long and steep hills to negotiate on what would be a tough, non-stop, 72-mile exhaustive push. Having once again courteously informed the various authorities and enlightened them as to the reason for my push, I was kindly encouraged by all concerned. I intended to start my mammoth push from the popular little resort of Menai, near its picturesque bridge that spanned the fast and turbulent waters of the infamous Menai straights. I contacted a police colleague at the strategic little town who I had known for many years, Constable Peter Powell. When the big day arrived, Peter and his Inspector kindly saw me off. I was followed by my little entourage, consisting of my back-up driver Matron in her car. Accompanying her was Mr Ali Boxie to film the event, which would be added to his previous footage of the Talacre push. Yet again, media coverage by the radio and local papers was to pay handsome dividends. People were waiting at their gates as I approached and each gave generously. Having previously spent many years holidaying on Anglesey with Marje and the children I was well aware of the calibre and generosity of the island's inhabitants. My travels manifested the wonderful, irreplaceable memories of days gone by. I found it very emotional when I passed the venues where Marje and I had spent many happy summer holidays in our little caravan. Being extremely sentimental I also suffer acute nostalgia. I pushed along enjoying the warm sun, continually reminiscing and reliving the times we had previously spent at the places I was passing. Eventually the sky clouded over and it began to rain. The rain gave me some cooling respite at first. Later, however, the heavens opened and I soon became soaked to the skin. It caused my wet hands to soften, which in turn caused blisters to appear and as the hours passed, my blisters burst and started to bleed. Eventually I reached the little paradise of Bull Bay. As I needed to tend to my hands, I decided to make an 'emergency pit stop'! We stopped at the Bull Bay Hotel where the kindly landlord cleaned and dressed my sore hands. Suitably cleaned, and refreshed with a glass of iced lemonade, I continued my journey up and out of Bull Bay towards Amlwch and distant Benllech. As I pushed I was continually handed donations by generous householders and motorists. Daylight eventually left me and the rains came and went as I headed through Amlwch. It was approaching midnight when I reached Benllech and here, as Matron's car continued to protect me from the rear, we were joined by a police car. This gave us added protection as we continued our progress along the dark, wet and desolate roads. The police car's powerful blue strobe lights flashed an eerie glow as their reflections, from the occasional shop windows, lit up the area. Finally, I reached Menai, my ultimate destination. I had completed a full circuit of the island, returning to where I had originally set off *twenty* long hours before. Our lonely little procession pulled in and stopped by the Bridge. Matron and the kindly policewoman prised my stiff form out of my chair, dried me then assisted me to change into dry clothing. We all then savoured a steaming hot cup of tea from the police officer's flask. I was extremely tired, but, totally elated. The push had been an absolute success. The kindly residents and motorists of Anglesey had donated over £600 to my bucket during my lengthy push. Again, further donations continued to be made to Clatterbridge due to the massive publicity this twenty hour, non-stop (except for the 'emergency' stop at Bull Bay) push had generated.

Although I did not anticipate repeating such a lengthy push as this again, I was now safe in the knowledge that I was well capable of pushing my heavy chair such durable distances, should I decide to do so in the future. I was *more* than happy with the successful outcome of my latest trek. Matron's pictures would definitely enhance my future talks and my bucket on the 'After Dinner' circuit.

Although I was physically very active with my pushes, my ongoing depression and deep grief remained with me. I was receiving counselling and my nurse regularly checked my amputation wound to ensure it was healing correctly. Also Reg, the vicar was still maintaining his caring visits to my home. Time was slowly moving on but my ever-present grief would never wane. My early morning visits to Marje continued unabated which allowed me the peace, solace and tranquillity I sought from my otherwise troubled emotions. I deliberately kept myself busy with ten or even twenty-mile pushes each and every day. Between or after my pushes I would be either writing or giving talks. The lifestyle I had adopted meant my troublesome and depressive lethargy was kept at bay. As well as my column in the *Wirral Champion* I was given yet another opportunity to increase my literary boundaries when

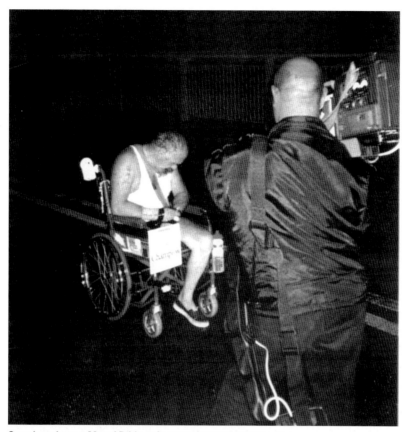

Swasie arrives at Menai Bridge after twenty hours and 72 miles.

I met a charming lady, Mrs Shirley Chisnall. Shirley was the editor of the emergency service's newspapers *Police Guardian* and *Fire Guardian*. On learning of my previous 'active, front line' experience in both services, Shirley kindly allowed me to write an article for each paper, based on my five years fire brigade and 27 years' police service experience. I jumped at the chance and my first articles duly appeared in each publication. These must have impressed her as I was then afforded my own column in each of the extremely popular and widely read papers. I was now a resident columnist in three prestigious publications. Never in my wildest dreams did I ever expect to reach such dizzy, journalistic heights. Each paper was highly respected and their distribution enjoyed a wide circulation throughout most of the United Kingdom. Instead of me being paid for my journalism, it was arranged that both of my editors would instead donate regularly to the Clatterbridge Cancer Charity. I was very happy with this arrangement as I could also give my fundraising activities added publicity. Shirley later fully took over the reins of proprietorship and launched the new *Police News* and *Fire News*, followed in turn by the *NHS News*. I now had columns in *four* 'upmarket' publications. Like the *Wirral Champion*, I didn't pull any punches and no doubt I am now the cause of Shirley's premature valium addiction!

Another lady friend, who was once the highest ranking policewoman in Great Britain, Alison Halford, contacted me and asked if I would like the chance to push my wheelchair through France. Obviously I jumped at the opportunity. Miss Halford had earlier acquired notoriety when she well and truly gave the government a 'bloody nose' at Strasburg. It was without doubt due to her court action that Britain's first female Chief Constable was appointed. I strongly recommend reading her book *No Way up the Greasy Pole* in which she describes in fascinating detail her adventurous 'altercation' and its cause, which led to her taking the government to Strasburg – and the cleaners!

I was invited to accompany 'Ma'am' to a family birthday party to be held at the little French resort of Fécamp. I certainly didn't wish to miss this opportunity so Miss Halford and I duly crossed the English Channel over to the continent. There, I raised a few francs by pushing from Dieppe along 80 miles of the French coastline to Fécamp. Once there we subsequently attended the lavish birthday 'bash'. Our host, another of Miss Halford's circle of friends, was none other than the father of the well-known television newsreader Penny Smith. The most enjoyable little soiree was held at the Smith family's hotel. After enjoying the wonderful party with its plentiful supply of lobster, crab and other equally fine cuisine, we concluded our week long stay on French soil. We thanked our warm, hospitable and extremely generous hosts before Miss Halford drove us both back to the ferry at Dieppe and over to England. On our return to 'Blighty' I duly changed the francs I had received into pounds, shillings and pence and topped up my bucket.

Later the same year, I attended the Police Convalescent Home at Auchterarder on the outskirts of Stirling in bonnie Scotland. My GP, Dr Smethurst, considered a therapeutic fortnight's stay there would do me the world of good. Accompanied by Matron I enjoyed a wonderful two-week convalescent stay at the first class, top of the range establishment for 'broken' bobbies up there in 'Haggisland'! During our most beneficial and enjoyable stay, the home's

Alison Halford when in ACC Merseyside Police.

Superintendent, the kindly Mr George Murray and his charming wife Jill, drove Matron and me to the Wallace (Braveheart) Monument at Stirling. The building was a magnificent, high, turreted stone structure over 150 feet high. Inside was a narrow, stone staircase similar to those in a church belfry. I enquired if I could ascend to the top with my chair and was politely told that this would be nigh impossible. I persisted with my request and eventually the doubting lady curator finally, and reluctantly, gave her permission for me to go ahead with my attempt! She promised me that if I succeeded in reaching the top I would not only be awarded a certificate, but I would also receive a modest donation to the Clatterbridge Fund. I then proceeded to take my trusty chair to its lofty pinnacle. After much grunting and groaning and after sustaining a few cuts and bruises, my scraped and battered chair and I reached the top of the mighty structure. There, Matron performed her usual ritual of photographing me sitting in my chair as I looked out towards the nearby Stirling Castle.

As well as my treasured certificate which authenticated a climb previously not thought possible, I was handed a donation to which Mr and Mrs Murray then kindly added, bringing a total of £50 for my bucket. The Scottish Press had a field day on learning of the most unusual event that had taken place at Stirling's world famous tourist attraction and this brought further revenue to my number one charity.

CHAPTER ELEVEN

The Pied Piper of Wirral

In September, another major event took place, when I was granted permission by the Isle of Man authorities to push my chair around the world famous TT motor cycle racing circuit. The distance of 38 miles included long and very steep hills which I would have to tackle. As Matron and I travelled over on the Sea Cat ferry from Liverpool, the ship's captain announced my intended charity push over the ship's PA system. Consequently I was inundated with donations from the benevolent passengers before I even set foot on the island. The Isle of Man Tourist Board, most admirably represented by Mrs Anna Hemmy, went to great lengths to assist and ensure it would be a total success. The emergency services all turned out to see me off on the memorable day and we had a press photo shoot before commencing the long push. Police, fire and ambulance personnel and their vehicles, together with a six-foot 'Viking' (a member of the tourist board staff) gathered before the cameras at the start. As always, Matron laboriously engaged herself photographing anything and everything throughout the whole of the nine-hour push. Donors materialised from pubs, shops, gardens and wherever people were gathered during my push under the day's hot, relentless sun. My police colleagues were fantastic; some of the off-duty officers escorted me for the duration of my physically demanding journey. Again, due to the wonderful assistance I received from everyone on the day, my bucket was filled to the brim. We later counted the money and cheques that had been so generously donated. The sum came to over £1,500. This included that which we had received on the outer ferry trip, but did not include the £200 plus, which we were to receive on our return journey!

My second lonely and bland Christmas passed by since the loss of Marje and I continued to fulfil my many engagements, to maintain a constant supply of 'pennies' for my cancer charity. I had by now, pushed my chair over 9,000 miles, during which time I had proudly increased the amount I had so far raised to well into five figures. During this time, I was invited to give a talk to a group of Rainbow Brownies at Maghull on the outskirts of Liverpool. The talk went well and my junior audience generously swelled my charity fund by the princely sum of £11.34. After my talk, as I sat among the children, consuming a welcome cuppa from Brown Owl, one of the children asked me if I lived in the country or near the sea. I told her that I lived near enough to both. The little Rainbow then asked if

Swasie at the start of the Isle of Man TT circuit, 38 miles.

I would take her and her friends out into the countryside one day. Consequently, with the enthusiastic collusion of Brown Owl, Guide Commissioner, Mrs Hilary Cockroft (an ex-schoolmate), the little Wirral town of West Kirby was visited by the Maghull troop of Rainbow Brownies. As the happy gang of girls alighted from the train at West Kirby station, boisterously squealing and screaming with delight, it looked like the sleepy little resort was being invaded by a 'platoon' from the famous, fictional school, Saint Trinians!

Brown Owl and her adult colleagues duly rounded up their 'troops' and we set off in a disciplined line along the footpaths of the Wirral Way, through the country park that was once the old steam railway route from Hooton to West Kirby. The children were delighted as they spotted various forms of wildlife, while they explored the leafy areas on a beautiful sunny day. One little girl, on spotting a bird with speckled plumage, heartily trilling its renditions for all to hear shouted, 'Oh look, that bird's got the measles!' She was promptly and authoritatively corrected by a little 'Jenny Know All' who informed her loudly, 'No it 'asn't, it's a Thrush!' Our adventurous trek took us on a couple of miles further before we stopped for a picnic. The children loved every minute. Moving on, we later wound our way around the outer expanse of the large marine lake. The little 'Jenny Know All' continued 'educating' all present by pointing out the various shells and marine life that were inhabiting the lake, rock pools and shoreline. Finally, the trek was concluded with ice creams at the little lakeside kiosk. After satisfying their gastronomic desires, the children sadly made their way back to the station to board their homeward bound train. They, and their adult escorts all enthusiastically stated that they had enjoyed an absolutely wonderful day 'over on the Wirral'. As the result of this day's excursion I received a telephone call inviting me to return to the Maghull Brownie's Headquarters. Mrs Cockroft informed me that as the children had not stopped talking about their 'fantastic day', their parents had held a collection and wished to donate this to my Clatterbridge Fund. On our return visit to Maghull, Matron and I were totally amazed when I was presented with a cheque for the staggering amount of £1,780.

In the months that followed, I visited the famous cooker manufacturers AGA, at their Telford factory in Shropshire. There, Matron and I were given a tour of the vast premises during which I made copious notes to furnish my forthcoming column in the *Wirral Champion*. As usual, I would illustrate my column with pictures that Matron was taking during our guided tour through the factory. When the article duly appeared in print, illustrated in colour, AGA were delighted. The result was that the benevolent AGA management contributed generously to the Clatterbridge Fund.

This gave me some audacious ideas of other ways to increase my wide circle of donors. I contacted Lomax, my wheelchair manufacturer at Dundee, informing them of the extraordinary 'feats' that their standard chair was successfully completing. The firm's

Swasie the Pied Piper with Maghull Brownies.

Managing Director, Mr John Wilmot, invited Matron and me to visit him at his factory, where he would show us around before kindly hosting us both to dinner and an overnight stay at a nearby hotel. The meeting was not only a resounding success for each of us but a deep and lifelong friendship was formed between Mr Wilmot, his family, Matron and me. Mr Wilmot was totally amazed at the achievements of his product. This first meeting was to fully enlighten him of the total success of each of his wheelchair product's endeavours, and to discuss my future intentions, wherever or whatever they may be. I was promised by an extremely impressed Mr Wilmot that he would guarantee his and his factory's assistance for any of my future charity activities should they be required. From that day forth, I was to enjoy a close relationship with Lomax of Dundee, now Sunrise Medical Limited, by projecting their name and their product's endurance capabilities. I started to assess and test their standard chairs as I travelled new frontiers in my ongoing quest to raise money for my cause. My travels involved negotiating tracks, heaths, commons and even shorelines, not the usual venues for such conveyances. I started to receive encouragement and valuable advice which continues unabated to this day.

I was now regularly being interviewed by, and appearing in, numerous high profile and famous magazines. My fees were gratefully received and donated to the charity. Regular radio and occasional TV appearances also continually enhanced the fund's finances.

I contacted Greater Manchester, Cheshire and Merseyside police forces to inform them of another non-stop long distance push of 60 miles from the Christie (Cancer) Hospital, Manchester to Clatterbridge Hospital, Wirral. As usual, the extremely helpful Chief Officers and their junior ranks were brilliant. Their much appreciated and generous assistance enabled me to successfully perform yet another demanding push which took 12 hours and 40 minutes of stamina-sapping energy to complete. The Manchester Police kept a beady eye on me as I left the confines of the Christie

'Swasie and his Lomax went all the way'

Mr Wilmot in Lomax boardroom.

Hospital in the dark, early hours of a quiet, wet Sunday morning. After two gruelling hours of pushing, I left the Greater Manchester area and entered Cheshire. I now had the advantage of daylight and could see the ever faithful Matron in my rear view mirror as she maintained station, a protective 50 yards behind me. Every now and again she would zoom ahead to take pictures before resuming her strategic position to my rear. The weather repeatedly changed as I made my laborious way along. One minute it would rain, then the sun would break through before more rain appeared. I was soaked, then dry, then soaked again! This was a hard push which included many hills. The texture of the road surface always played a part too.

The rougher the surface, the more difficult it was for my casters and hands. When it was wet my hands became soft, when it was dry my hands maintained their texture of leather. Many long and weary hours later I thankfully left Cheshire and entered the county of Merseyside. I now felt I was nearing 'home' as I pushed along the busy and familiar A-41 trunk road. As always, radio coverage maintained a constant stream of donations from the kind motorists who, having heard of the push on their car radios, would stop and hand me money as well as drinks and chocolate.

As darkness descended I was now six miles (nearly two hours) from my goal. A Merseyside Police patrol car drew alongside me and checked that I was well. The crew complimented me on my many bright red rear lights (as well as the front two white lights) saying that they 'could see me for miles'. With renewed confidence and my morale boosted by my colleagues' presence, I plodded on and eventually reached Clatterbridge Hospital at Bebington. On my arrival I received an unexpected and tumultuous welcome from the hospital staff, nurses, doctors and patients – and of course the press. A foil thermal blanket was placed around my shoulders by a concerned nurse and Matron and I were given a most welcome cup of tea.

Although I was elated at the successful conclusion of my lengthy push, I was also choked when I learned that some of those who had taken the trouble to welcome me were terminally ill cancer patients. They had come from their wards specially to see me arrive. Gestures like this *never* ceased to make me feel very humble. I felt unbelievably privileged to be in such company.

During my endeavours, whether they be pushes or talks, I always find the people to be respectfully considerate. They always show courtesy and are aware of the fact that people in wheelchairs tend to have obvious 'disadvantages'. However, as time goes on, I *never* cease to wonder at the attitude of some folk. Although, during my lifetime I have 'been round the block' a few times, I am still continually surprised at the amount of people who are either quite unconcerned

Swasie near the end of his 60-mile push from Christie Hospital to Clatterbridge, twelve hours and 40 minutes.

about, or totally oblivious of, the disabled fraternity. Many show total disrespect or are just plain ignorant or selfish by solely thinking of themselves. These people just do not give a monkey's for their fellow members of society. Often when I try to open a door to enter a shop or negotiate steps into a building, I find people stand idly by, staring. Many times I have experienced this and many times I make my sentiments known. I can't resist saying loudly, 'It's okay, you just stand there, I can manage!' to ensure that all who are near hear my dulcet tones of frustrated and angry dissent. As I have previously stated, the 'does he take sugar' syndrome is always prevalent. The total opposite is the case when I see people with various physical or learning difficulties in the company of their professional carers. Then, they are courteously assisted, or spoken to as an *individual* person. This is what should be expected from everyone.

Although I have come to terms with my own disability and I am fiercely independent, I do (and always will) take up the cudgels and fight for the rights of those who are disabled or physically or mentally handicapped. This will continue to take any form I deem appropriate to safeguard or improve the interests of those I consider are not being suitably catered for. I started this particular 'crusade' after my experience during the Wirral Coastal Walk when I had been courteously told that it was a charity event for people to *walk* the fifteen miles for their individual charities. It was pointed out to me that the 'Wirral Way' part of the walk, through the country park area was not 'suitable' for wheelchairs due to narrow paths, gateways and stiles. I pig-headedly insisted that I be allowed to take part in the event, which ultimately I completed.

However, this was not without mishap as the reader will remember! My point is, after the event I never stopped bleating to all and sundry that such events as the Wirral Coastal Walk should not be out of bounds to those who are unfortunate enough to be in a wheelchair. I like to think that my efforts brought results. Whether or not they did I don't know, but I can say that the beautiful, panoramic views of the river Dee shoreline and North Wales coast can now be enjoyed by all. The Wirral Way has now become totally 'wheelchair friendly'. This stunning scenic route can be enjoyed by cyclists, horse riders, ramblers and – people in wheelchairs! The council authorities responsible for this should certainly be given a well deserved accolade for bringing this about.

In an effort to enhance the funds for my number one charity, I had applied to enter the 1998, extremely prestigious and world famous London Marathon Fun Run. When I applied to the marathon authorities I fully explained that my wheelchair was just a bog standard NHS chair with little front casters. My sole purpose was to take part and complete the 26-mile event to raise as much money as possible. However my application was refused. I made enquiries as to why I had been turned down and I eventually spoke to a Mr Alan Storey. He curtly informed me that I would not be able to take part as I would be a 'danger' to his elite runners and wheelchair racers. I emphasised to Mr Storey that in no way did I wish to enter the 'Wheelchair Race'; I only wished to take part in the 'Fun' run and raise money for my charity. My pleading fell on deaf ears and I was abruptly informed by Mr Storey that my entry would not be accepted. The *able-bodied* Mr Storey went on to inform me that he considered that I would be physically unable to complete 26 miles in such a conveyance. He elaborated by (correctly) pointing out that such a chair as mine was only constructed and intended for use around the house or wards, or perhaps a gentle push to the shops. So what? I pointed out to Mr Storey that I had previously completed non-stop distances well in excess of 26 miles on many occasions, over all sorts of difficult terrain in the same chair. Again, my reasoning fell on deaf ears. As much as Mr Storey was determined to keep me out, I was just as determined that one day I would enter and successfully complete the so far elusive London Marathon. I was so angry at my rebuff that I informed the press and my impolite refusal was subsequently splashed all over the papers. The publicity brought about a BBC interview when I again explained my reasons for entering the Marathon with my standard chair. Not only did I wish to raise funds, but I also hoped that my efforts would be an inspiration to other 'ordinary' wheelchair users. Although my interview was on tape, when this was subsequently broadcast, Mr Storey was live in the studio and able to have his say but I obviously couldn't reply. Due to the furore I caused, I was assisted by others to enter, namely Sir Jimmy Saville, the late Sports Minister Mr Tony Banks and his successor Kate Hoey. A local veteran marathon runner offered his supportive rhetoric on air and in the press. Our joint efforts got us exactly nowhere!

By hook or by crook, I would make damned sure my trusty

chariot and I *would* complete the 26-mile London Marathon one day. I continued on with my talks and pushes, and visits were maintained by my nurse, counsellors and 'Uncle Tom Cobley an' all'! Due to my persistent daily wheelchair pushes my mileage was accumulating at an amazing degree.

I now started an insatiable affair with the Fire Services National Benevolent Fund. I would regularly attend and assist at fire station car washes to raise funds for the 'Ben Fund' as it is known. My efforts to assist them were reciprocal. Members of the fire services are an extremely charitable bunch; always willing to assist my fundraising efforts. I sought after, and was granted permission to visit every Merseyside fire station where I would ascend each tower. There were a large number of stations to cover as Merseyside Fire Brigade now included some of Cheshire County Brigade's fire stations, namely Heswall, Runcorn and Bebington. I started my trek at Southport fire station and eventually pushed to all of the Merseyside stations – and, climbed their towers. This totalled a staggering 120 miles over a period of four days. I was greeted at some of the stations by local dignitaries, the press and sometimes the Mayor of the area I visited. The massive publicity that ensued was equalled by the massive generosity of the people of Merseyside.

The generosity of those truly wonderful people of Southport, Liverpool and Wirral absolutely knew no bounds. The first morning of my endeavour brought about an act of extreme benevolence. As I pushed from Southport towards Crosby in company with a brigade Sub Officer, a Rolls Royce pulled in front of us and glided to a stop. The driver, (a well known businessman in the area) then got out of his vehicle and handed the astonished Sub Officer a £50 note. The man shook both our hands telling us he had heard about us on his car radio earlier that day. He then returned to his car and drove off leaving the two of us gobsmacked! I can't quite remember the amazed words of gratitude the gruff, streetwise, most esteemed Sub Officer uttered. I think his words were something like, 'Flipping heck Swasie, I do declare, he's just given us 50 blooming quid!' I later sent the extremely generous and modest donor (who I won't name) a copy of my book *Off the Cuff* as a token of my gratitude.

The rest of the day went well and we accomplished what we had set out to do. Even though it was only a few miles from home, I decided for convenience, to accept the warm hospitality of station accommodation as this would maintain continuity the following morning. Sometimes children walked alongside me and my fire engine escort through the streets of Bootle, Liverpool and parts of Wirral. The amount of money that filled the buckets was nothing short of amazing. The Mayor and Mayoress of Wirral gave a substantial sum when they greeted me at Upton Fire Station on the outskirts of Birkenhead. The funds were swelled by a further generous donation from the Fire Chief and his senior officers. I would ensure that as well as the Cancer Fund, the coffers of the Ben Fund would be considerably increased by my efforts in the future. I intended to complete *many* fundraising endeavours specifically for the Ben Fund.

The many pictures taken of this event were again subsequently entered and included in my talks. When Matron was unable to accompany me, as in the case of the fire stations push, I would ensure that whoever accompanied me was able to make a pictorial record of the event, specifically for inclusion in my fundraising talks. Without doubt, the pictures had the desired effect of ensuring attention to those I was addressing. Some of the pictures shown to my audiences, young and old, were almost guaranteed to produce the financial response I so eagerly and relentlessly sought for my ever hungry charity bucket. When Matron's duties as a highly efficient store detective and 'thief taker' allowed, I knew I could depend on her high quality, dramatic pictures to elaborate my verbal ramblings to the varied gatherings I regularly stood (sat!) in front of.

I was interviewed yet again by another universally-read magazine, the prestigious *Woman's Own* where a tender and moving feature was written and suitably illustrated by one of Matron's pictures. Again this brought roadside responses, encouraging comments and generous donations from those who were obviously ardent readers of *Woman's Own*. I also enjoyed my now, regular scheduled visits to numerous local schools. I am always very impressed with the courteous receptions I receive at these establishments. I am also grateful for such keen and polite interest shown by the pupils during my talks. I was now being invited to such venues as tightly-packed front rooms of houses, where local housewives get together to find out what my adventures are all about. I am always pleasantly surprised at the generous amounts raised at these small events.

I was now also enjoying further privileges by being invited to coffee by the Mayors of Wirral and Lord Mayors of Liverpool. Similar invitations were also kindly afforded me by the Chief Constable and Fire Chief of Merseyside. Realising the potential of exceedingly good PR for all of my hosts, I would ensure to generate this at every opportunity during appropriate future events.

My utter devotion to my cause was kindly rewarded when I received a wonderful and unexpected accolade from the 'people of Wirral'. I was voted 'Wirral Volunteer of the Year' in 1999. I was tremendously proud at this and immediately dedicated the award to my Marje in whose memory all of my endeavours are relentlessly carried out. Matron, my daughter Jo and myself proudly attended the award ceremony where I was presented with a beautiful trophy, which now proudly adorns my mantelpiece.

One day whilst I was out pushing along the local roads I was approached by a gentleman cyclist who stopped to ask how I was. He went on to explain that he too was 'travelling the same road' of inconsolable grief. The gentleman, Mr Malcolm Creek informed me that his daughter, Alison, had sadly succumbed to leukaemia at the young age of 23 years, a couple of years before. I could tell by Mr Creek's emotional demeanour how painful it was as he spoke about her. Although I never had the privilege of meeting Alison, I certainly sympathised and fully understood what poor Mr Creek was going through. Mr Creek informed me that he and his wife Gillian had organised a forthcoming 'Bikeathon' in memory of their daughter. The event was to raise much needed funds to assist research into the equally merciless killer, Leukaemia. Without hesitation, I volunteered to take part and assist his extremely worthy cause.

The Bikeathon would be a 26-mile trip in the form of a figure of eight. After completing thirteen miles the participant would arrive back at the starting point and would then carry on and perform another figure of eight out into the 'sticks', before returning again to the original starting venue. The second figure of eight would encompass calling at Clatterbridge Cancer Hospital. Although Mr Creek appreciated my offer of assistance, he politely pointed out that it was a 26-mile *cycle* event which would be completed well before I had even pushed around the first leg. I appreciated the gentleman's advice but I was determined to complete the whole 26-mile course to help Mr and Mrs Creek's efforts.

Although the morning of the event started wet and windy there was no shortage of enthusiastic cyclists, of all ages. It was pointed out that anyone wishing to just complete the first half (thirteen miles) could do so and they would still receive a medal. We all set off from alongside the well-known Arrowe Park golf club on the outskirts of Birkenhead. There were well in excess of 700 cyclists. Some were on tandems, some were even towing small children in covered trailers. From the very outset a carnival atmosphere prevailed and everyone was most enthusiastic to assist. Some of the push involved rough terrain and steep hills but I negotiated the first half without any trouble. After successfully completing the first thirteen miles Mr and Mrs Creek caringly suggested that I should leave it at that, as most had already completed the whole 26-mile course. I thanked them both for their concern but wouldn't hear of it. Subsequently, after a further lengthy and exhaustive push, I completed the second circuit and eventually concluded my push back at Arrowe Park. It was raining when I arrived and 'returned to the fold'. Although I arrived hours after the last cyclist, this did not prevent Mr and Mrs Creek and a couple of St John Ambulance officers hanging around in the rain to afford me an extremely warm welcome. Mrs Creek thoroughly congratulated me and after she retrieved a ribbon bearing an attractive medal from a nearby table, I then enjoyed the ultimate, proud privilege of her placing it around my neck. Due entirely to this brilliant idea from Mr and Mrs Creek, and the extremely kind and benevolent donations from the people of Wirral, many of whom so enthusiastically took part on the day, over £23,000 was raised for the Leukaemia Research Fund.

CHAPTER TWELVE

More Blissful Ignorance

My nocturnal visits to Marje and daily pushes continued to increase the already high numbers on my mileometer considerably. Radio interviews and regular mentions in the local papers maintained not only a high profile, but the fuel of publicity meant that a constant flow of donations to my bucket was maintained whatever I did or wherever I went. The saying, 'Great oak trees from little acorns grow' was to prove true. Soon, a major development would be conceived from a simple, but as it would turn out, *very* important, visit I was invited to attend!

I received a 'phone call from Mr Wilmot at Lomax inviting Matron and me to attend a 'Mobility Roadshow' at Crowthorne near Reading. As I was more or less the unofficial wheelchair 'Test Pilot' for Lomax, as Mr Wilmot put it, he went on to explain that his firm were to display various Lomax products to the manufacturing fraternity of disability aids and equipment. Mr Wilmot also wanted to show off a Lomax product (my standard wheelchair) that he was convinced was completely 'out gunning' *any* Lomax competition.

By this time Matron, as she lived 25 miles from me, would regularly stay at my house for convenience when we needed to travel long distances to events. Consequently, Matron and I travelled to Reading where we met Mr Wilmot and his staff at their Lomax stand. I was asked to push my chair about the vast area of the complex during the three-day event, to display my chair – the chair that Mr Wilmot had previously informed all and sundry had completed numerous lengthy pushes across varied forms of terrain. He had ensured that many of those at the Mobility Roadshow were already aware of my unusual feats and climbs in the standard Lomax product. I audaciously did as I was told and hovered near and alongside the stands of Lomax competitors, pretending I was just looking at their products. I also took down copies of *Wheelchair Pilot* to place on the Lomax stand. This was a glossy, illustrated publication completed and published by my editor Mr John Bertwistle of the *Wirral Champion*. It contained a chronology of my wheelchair endeavours, dramatic pictures, a selection of my 'Sir Upsetting' columns and some of my paintings and cartoons. The book is a very eye catching item by its uniquely illustrated cover. Many of the visitors not only perused its pages but also purchased copies. On seeing me, the man on the cover, some would stop me to chat about what they had just been reading. One of these was a Miss Lou Birks. Miss Birks was visiting the show with a television camera crew, where they were filming the latest various products to benefit those with disabilities for a future television documentary programme.

Miss Birks visited the Lomax stand where she scrutinised the pages of *Wheelchair Pilot*. When she had finished she spoke to Mr Wilmot about his firm's product referred to in the book. Mr Wilmot then introduced me to the lady and we had an interesting chat about the things I was getting up to in my Lomax chair. Miss Birks then asked me, 'What would be your ultimate ambition to do in that chair?' I informed her that I would love to push my chair from John O'Groats to Land's End. My comments brought ribald laughter from those present. Miss Birks then said, 'Oh come on, I'm being serious, what would you *really* like to do in that chair?' I quickly replied, 'I've just told you, I'd like to push from John O'Groats to Land's End'. Miss Birks went on to inform me that it would not be physically possible to push such a castered chair for that distance. I argued that it would and confidently emphasised, 'If I had a vehicle behind me with a bottle of water and some jam butties I would do it!' Standing pensively nearby deeply in thought, with one hand cupping his chin and the other arm folded across his barrel-like chest, Mr Wilmot said slowly, for all to hear, 'If you had a back up vehicle, would you *really*

The Mobility Roadshow, with Mr Wilmot and his Lomax team.

do it Swasie?'‘Bloody right I would’, I replied. Having very carefully considered what had been said, Mr Wilmot then responded with, ‘Okay Swasie, I will provide the vehicle and driver to accompany you if you really *are* serious’! I quickly confirmed that I had never been more serious in my life. To the amazement of the doubting Miss Birks, and those others within earshot, the first ever standard NHS End-to-End wheelchair push was born. I was absolutely ecstatic with joy. My wheelchair climbs and pushes had finally led me to what would be the ultimate of all firsts – pushing my standard Lomax chair, unaided, the whole length of Great Britain from John O’Groats to Land’s End, the ‘Holy Grail’ of all marathon efforts.

Again, many 'doubting Thomases' expressed their lack of belief that this could be done in such a conveyance. However, they hadn't taken into consideration the fact that my Marje is, and will always be, my total inspiration. In no way would failure be an option. I envisaged that such a push would raise an astronomical sum of money for charity if everything was done and thought out properly. In the weeks that followed, John Wilmot and I burned a lot of midnight oil as we pedantically discussed the logistics of such a major undertaking.

As I was an ex-firefighter, I decided to contact every fire brigade from John O'Groats to Land's End whose area I would pass through. Many audacious negotiations ensued during the following months. Requests to each Chief Officer would have to be made seeking their assistance and blessing. Overnight accommodation, and food if possible, would be sought at fire stations en-route. This would involve contacting the many retained (part time) personnel, which in itself would be no easy task due to their full time roles. This illustrates the administrative complexity involved in the arranging of such a high profile venture, which, let us not forget, would entail travelling through *two* countries! Chief police officers would also have to be contacted and informed of the little 'posse' that would be wending its way through their 'patches'. This would be absolutely necessary both as a matter of etiquette and courtesy, as well as seeking their blessing and much valued help and guidance. All in all, preparing for such a trek as this, as well as the logistical operation involved, would be no easy task for all concerned. Safety must and would be paramount at all times. I also sought the invaluable expertise and assistance of the 'Land's End to John O'Groats Company', the official body concerned in the authenticating of such marathons undertaken from End-to-End. I was confident that a lot of money would be raised, and wanted to divide this equally between Clatterbridge Cancer and the Fire Services National Benevolent Fund. During my keen preparations for the End-to-End push I still maintained the rigorous programme of my other commitments. I had the honour and privilege of leading a carnival procession, accompanied by the Mayor of Wirral and the cavalry of the elite Merseyside Police Mounted department. The day went well and the weather ensured that everyone enjoyed the facilities at Heswall's 'Puddydale' ground as they meandered around the stalls, coconut shies and various other entertainments. The day raised a lot of funds for various charities, including my own.

The next major event to follow was the prestigious 'Wirral Show'. I attended the Wirral Champion stand in company with my editor, the magazine's proprietor Mr John Birtwistle. There I met an old friend Lynda Chalker (now Baroness Chalker) who purchased a copy of *Wheelchair Pilot*. A brilliant display was given by the world famous Red Arrows in their bright red Hawk trainers. This was followed by various vintage aircraft giving an equally appreciated appearance. Matron and I again visited bonnie Scotland to attend a photo shoot on the banks of Loch Earn to enhance the Lomax profile. As well as Mr Wilmot, bearing the cost of our hotel stay and the cost of our fuel, he kindly gave a donation to my cancer bucket. This type of gesture is typical of the extremely benevolent Mr Wilmot. I enlisted the sponsorship of many small and large firms and establishments to assist in one way or another the forthcoming End-to-End push. These included the massive resources of Duracell Batteries, Fuji Films, Jabra Europe, Vauxhall Motors, Greentyre, Lucozade and Liptonice Tea, Berghaus, Convetech Medical Supplies, Tempormed Medical Products, AGA, Halfords Cycles, Cateye – Zero, Greentyre (whose unchanged tyres would cushion my journey for the duration) as well as many local small businesses in the Wirral area. The list of those who were prepared to back me became endless. Also, I must not forget all those generous people, including schoolchildren, who regularly stop me in all weathers irrespective of whether I am officially collecting or not.

Another engagement I had the privilege of being invited to perform was the opening of a Red Cross charity shop in Bebington, Wirral. Although a small function, I was nevertheless extremely honoured at being asked to perform the opening ceremony. A few weeks later, after consulting with H.M. Coastguard, I pushed my chair on what was my hardest trek so far. Together with a film camera crew sitting precariously on the tail gate of the Country Warden's Landrover, I somehow managed to propel, drag, push, and pull my 47lb chariot across the three miles of mud, sand, rocks and gullies of the Dee Estuary to Hilbre Island. I set out at 2.00pm and after much grunting and sweating, my soaking wet, mud-caked frame eventually arrived on the island. After a welcome cuppa at the warden's cottage we returned to shore, arriving back at our starting point at 8.15pm. The day's fundraising effort raised £4.97p from two kindly 'twitchers' on the island. However, due to heavy press coverage after the event Clatterbridge was to benefit enormously.

My 'after dinner' functions continued together with my ongoing columns for the *Police* and *Fire News*, *Wirral Champion* and my next book! As well as the heavy ink consumption of my quill, the preparations continued smoothly for the End-to-End push, which was as yet still some time away.

Each year the police forces of Europe stage a big event called the 'Windsor Walk'. This is a walk of either fifteen or 25 miles and is open to all police and ex-police officers from European countries. Completion of the 25 miles wins a gold medal; completing the fifteen miles wins a silver. I decided to enter this very prestigious event, as I was almost certain that completing this with Matron would enhance the cancer fund considerably. So Matron and I applied to take part. I was immediately informed that in no way would a wheelchair be able to enter. It was tactfully explained that the footpaths were too narrow and the terrain would be too difficult to negotiate. I insisted that I be able to take part, and finally I was able to persuade the authorities who, although reluctantly, allowed my application. The event started at Egham University and continued over a footbridge and out into the countryside. The large crowd set off up the University steps, then across the road via an iron footbridge, then down a steep, narrow path into heavy undergrowth.

Swasie setting off to Hibre Island in the Dee Estuary.

The authorities were quite right; it was obvious that this was not in any way a wheelchair event. From the start, even Matron doubted whether I would even complete half the distance. Not to be thwarted, I pig-headedly intended to complete the whole 26 miles, whatever it took!

In no time the demanding environment started to take its toll. I had to force my way through bushes, nettles and thorns before falling headlong into a ditch. Although help was offered I managed to 'remount' and carry on, but I again repeatedly came out of my chair when the casters cut into the soil or wet grass. It was indeed true; the paths were too narrow for the chair's wheels. It was only by holding onto the thorny blackberry bushes with one hand, as I propelled my chair along the banks of the river Thames, that I prevented myself falling into the river. As the event was held yearly there were concrete steps that were hardly used, except when this event took place. The steps were sharp enough to cut and graze my back and leg as well as weeds and nettles that grew amongst them. In no time I was stung, bitten by hordes of insects and scratched by thorns, but I would not quit.

During the push the rains came with a vengeance. After enjoying the comforts of a metal road up past Windsor Castle, Matron and I walked the 'Long Mile' (three miles on the straight) through Windsor Park where the rain totally drenched us both. I was fortunate as I was only clad in vest and shorts; poor Matron was wearing everything but the kitchen sink, yet she was soaked to the skin. At the end of the Long Mile was the culmination of the 15-mile walk, the silver medal. My thoroughly soaked and dejected partner decided to call it a day at this point. She was taken to a nearby tent to dry and change; hopefully the clothes in her backpack would not be soaked also. I stubbornly continued on now devoid of company.

I had to ask a park employee the way to the next marshal at one stage. The rain continued to fall in sheets. I eventually entered thick forest foliage and in no time I was completely lost. As I headed on slowly and with difficulty I spotted a number of chestnuts all over the forest floor. As I had a plastic carrier bag under my seat I decided to fill this and take them back for the children at Claire House, a children's hospice adjacent to Clatterbridge Hospital. As I foraged amongst the undergrowth I soon harvested my bag with lots of enormous conkers for the kids. I was delighted. Now then! My next challenge would be to get myself out of the woods and back on track, but this would be easier said than done. Fortunately I heard voices, then Matron's dulcet tones as she repeatedly shouted my name. 'Over here!' I shouted. Soon, the bushes in front of me parted and there was Matron, accompanied by two men who were sergeants from the Royal Protection squad. When I asked Matron to carry my bag of

The 'Long' Windsor Mile.

conkers, she uttered some expletives which caused even the two hardened sergeants to blush! Eventually I persuaded Matron to relieve me of my bag containing half of the forest's conkers!

Matron informed me that the two sergeants insisted on putting my chair into their vehicle when we reached the road and they would then transport me the rest of the way back. I blatantly refused, telling them that I intended to complete the whole 25 miles 'under my own steam'! This did not please the two sergeants one bit. One of them replied sternly, 'You'll do as you're told'! I immediately informed him that during the whole of my lengthy police service I hardly did as I was told and I wasn't going to start now! After being successfully placed back on course I continued my push for the remainder of the route. I stubbornly persevered and eventually managed to return to Egham University in the dark, hours after everyone else, having completed an extra mile due to my getting lost in the forest. The whole of the day's participants nevertheless waited for my arrival and congratulated me on my effort and filled my bucket until it was overflowing! The day's endeavour was a total but extremely exhaustive success. I had a 'field day' writing about the 'Windsor Walk' in my columns. I must confess, in hindsight, the authorities were totally correct; the Windsor Walk is definitely not suitable for participants in wheelchairs, as almost the whole course is wheelchair unfriendly and in parts, dangerous. However, this major event was an endeavour that could not help but prepare me for the lengthy End-to-End push that awaited me in the coming months.

Yet another 'first' came about when I attended a film and photo shoot at Birkenhead Bus Depot. *Wheelchair Pilot* was advertised by being prominently displayed on the sides of the Birkenhead area buses, and a camera crew wished to film this to include amongst their previous documentary footage. It was at this time that I became interested in raising funds for the South Atlantic Medal Association (SAMA 82). This is a charity that caters for veterans of the 1982 Falklands conflict. I have a friend who served on the islands during their subsequent successful recovery from the Argentine invaders.

Swasie lost in Windsor Park during the Windsor Walk.

I was keen to assist the fund, so I contacted the fund authorities and volunteered to retrace the route our forces took across East Falkland, from Ports San Carlos to Stanley, a distance of 72 miles over the extremely rugged and mountainous terrain. I was politely listened to but my offer was deemed somewhat 'far fetched'! I eventually convinced SAMA that not only was I extremely serious but that I would actually complete the journey. After many long and detailed discussions regarding travel, and accommodation, the sceptical ex-Falklands Para veteran Denzil Connick, Secretary of SAMA 82, and his equally sceptical veteran colleagues and I agreed that the event would take place in November 2000. The push would end at the war memorial, Stanley at 11.00am on the eleventh day of the eleventh month. My heart pounded at the thought of being granted such and ultimate honour and privilege.

As well as the thoughts of this future endeavour crowding my head, things were by now also very much on course for the John O'Groats saga, which I awaited with enthusiasm and a little trepidation. My 'after dinner' status was elevated somewhat as talks now included giving an address at two extremely prestigious venues; those of Tranmere Rovers and Liverpool Football clubs – I was moving up in the world! Another proud moment was also achieved; my third book, *Onto the Final Leg* had just been successfully published. Marje would be so proud! I also started training with Vic Charles at Radio Clatterbridge to become a hospital radio presenter. As with my editors, I was soon to become the cause of Vic's premature Valium addiction!

As much as enjoying my various efforts and endeavours which gave me a lot of proud satisfaction, I was still experiencing the inconsiderate attitude of those who persisted in being rude and offensive to those with various forms of physical difficulties. I continually experienced people letting doors go in my face or standing in front of me at shows (even sometimes with children on their shoulders), exhibitions or just ignorantly pushing in front of my chair or leaning over me in shops. My patience was being constantly tested to the limit. When I see strangers who are in a similar position to myself being shown discourtesy or rudeness, I will immediately jump in and inform such perpetrators the error of their ways. Scenes like this are sadly an everyday occurrence. How different things are when I visit or address schools or colleges. Then the complete opposite is always the case. I continue to find that children and young people always tend to show more disability awareness, and can certainly teach their adult peers much in society's field of tolerance and courtesy. Authorities too must bear a lot of responsibility regarding welfare and consideration towards those who are disabled. Much more needs to be done in the name of progress before such conduct and problems, such as I have mentioned, can be addressed satisfactorily. I intend to maintain my enthusiastic monitoring of this unsatisfactory and ongoing difficulty, however unpopular my actions or writing may be, in bringing these matters to the notice of those 'Mandarins' in the corridors of power!

CHAPTER THIRTEEN

A New Millennia

The end of 1999 arrived and another Christmas, still devoid of any feeling of festivity, came and went. Now we were into the year 2000, which also began a new century. Coincidentally, my first book, *Off the Cuff* (my illustrated autobiography) was to be printed again – for the *third* time. I proudly realised what a privileged achievement it was to have one of my books published in *two* separate millennia!

My ongoing fundraising endeavours now also included me concentrating on the arrangements for the John O'Groats push in a few months' time. Mr Wilmot and his Lomax team, assisted by Duracell, were hard at work organising their own arrangements. I busied myself contacting the various police forces and fire brigades to enlighten them all as to my intended route and requirements. I received nothing but the utmost courteous assistance and guidance from all concerned. This reinforced my fierce, devoted pride at being part of such an elite 'brotherhood'. I intended to show my gratitude by ensuring my efforts generated the maximum PR for all the brigades and police forces whose 'territory' I passed through. My time was also consumed with talks at schools and charity gatherings and my daily mileage continued uninterrupted. The build-up to the event consisted of TV, radio and press interviews which, even *before* the event, started to bring about a lot of donations. I had intended to leave John O'Groats on Marje's birthday, the 12th May, but due to a talk having been arranged prior to the push's conception at Crowthorne, it was decided to postpone the push for one week.

After a massive, televised send off from the Lomax factory at Dundee, during which I was waved off by the Lady Provost of the

City, together with Mr Wilmot, his wife Careen and the directors and workers from the factory, my backup man Art Sangster drove me on to distant Wick, 250 miles away. There we would stay overnight at the little village's fire station before moving on up to John O'Groats the following day to commence the 'journey of a lifetime'.

After a night's sleep on the recreation room floor alongside the station snooker table, our departure from the tip of Scotland started on a very wet and windy morning. The first day's push went well and after yet another overnight stay at Wick, I plodded on southwards, escorted for the first two miles by a fire engine from Wick. Each day was an adventure and once out in the wild but beautiful countryside, the only company I had was my Lomax escort 500 yards behind, some highland cattle and the occasional sight of a Golden Eagle. The Scottish wildlife was phenomenal and fascinating. Like Matron, Art too was a keen photographer, and *never* missed an opportunity to record all on film, which had been generously donated for this purpose by Fuji. The days went by and the push through the meteorologically temperamental highlands was hard due to the steep, mountainous gradients I had to negotiate. Even though traffic was light at first, motorists stopped to give generously. The crofters also donated benevolently as I passed their quaint little thatched, white stone cottages. Art and I were blessed with meeting a very generous lady, Mrs Ann Matheson, the owner of the little Tea Room in the picturesque village of Glencoe, whose customers include the well-known charity fundraiser Sir Jimmy Saville. Our temporary hostess made sure Art and I were more than adequately fed and watered when we stopped at her neat little establishment. Not only did this kind lady feed us for free, she later drove after us up into the mountains to give us a generous cash donation for our bucket from her and her customers. Mrs Matheson is typical of those wonderful highland people who never hesitate to give so generously. So much for the traditional view of Scottish people being mean!

During the days that followed I saw many wonderful sights during my travels through beautiful Scotland. I also had many

Swasie being seen off by colleagues from John O'Groats.

adventures and met lots of extremely nice people, many of whom were to remain lasting friends. After seventeen long days, I finally left Scotland behind and entered England at Gretna Green. My lengthy push through and down the rest of England was equally enjoyable but hard. The mammoth push was finally and successfully concluded at Land's End, 44 long and exhaustive days after setting off from far away John O'Groats. During the length of the push over £14,000 was raised (which Art Sangster pedantically banked en route). The eventual total was over £23,000 which was then divided equally between the Clatterbridge Cancer Fund and the Fire Services National Benevolent Fund.

I wrote down all my memories of this dramatic journey and had them published in a book called *Tip to Toe*. This was illustrated with all the wonderful images that Art and Matron took along the way. I was also lucky to have a foreword written by Dame Tanni Grey-Thompson, the Olympic, wheelchair gold medallist. *Tip to Toe*, like my previous books, has been a great success.

During the End-to-End push my backup and I were hosted and accommodated at many fire stations. One such station was in the beautiful Cornish town of Bodmin. There, amongst my brilliant and extremely hospitable hosts, I met a man who was to become a close, lifelong friend, Richard Helleur. It so happened that Richie too was

Swasie completes the End-to-End push at Land's End.

an ex-Para (Parachute Regiment) and 1982 Falklands war veteran. Obviously we discussed the Falklands and on my mentioning my intended 'Tab' across the island in my wheelchair, Richie commented on how he would 'give his all' to accompany me. In 1982, as two young Bodmin Paras, Richie and his close friend Mark Holman-Smith had left the safe confines of Bodmin to go and fight a war on the inhospitable Falkland Islands, 8,000 miles away in the South Atlantic Ocean. Sadly, Mark was killed during the fighting for Goose Green and Richie returned to Bodmin alone. I decided to see what I could do to enable Richie to accompany me as my 'carer'. Due to the notoriety and subsequent large donations the 'Groats' push generated, I enjoyed direct access to the 'Top Brass' of the police and fire services.

The first thing I did was contact the secretary of SAMA, Denzil Connick, to 'sound out' the prospect of Richie's return to the Falklands as my backup and 'carer'. The result was that SAMA expressed their enthusiastic delight to facilitate his return. They accepted that his return may not only be therapeutic for him in the elimination of any 'gremlins' he may still have, but also, he would be an invaluable 'carer' for his wheelchair prodigy. Once SAMA had given the green light, I then sought permission from Richie's top boss, the brigade's Chief Fire Officer, Mike Howells. Mr Howells' instant response was brilliant. Provided Richie's trip did not interfere with any brigade requirements or the annual leave arrangements of his colleagues, permission was granted. Richie was ecstatic at the thought of his return and I too was absolutely delighted. The Falkland Islands wheelchair push with a Para 'escort' was born. Many times Richie would enquire and comment as to how on earth I would be able to complete such an overland push in a wheelchair. I must admit that I too was secretly apprehensive, however, I was determined that this venture would be successfully completed. The push would undoubtedly be a major undertaking as nothing like this had ever been contemplated before, never mind being physically undertaken. Despite my concerns, I was jubilant and extremely confident. I also knew that with Richie alongside me, the Falklands 'Mission' couldn't fail!

Six weeks before the forthcoming Falklands trip Matron and I, together with Miss Jan Hayes, the Clatterbridge Cancer Charity Secretary, attended the official John O'Groats to Land's End cheque presentation at the Lomax factory in Dundee. Lady Provost of Dundee presented the cheques to Miss Hayes for the Clatterbridge Cancer charity, and Assistant Divisional Officer Ian Bennett for the Fire Services National Benevolent Fund. The ceremony was attended by the whole of the Lomax staff and factory workforce and headed by Mr and Mrs Wilmot and senior members of Duracell. The event was given much publicity by the press which in turn brought about further donations. A further ceremony concerning the push would also be arranged; this time the venue would be at the opposite end of the country, namely the famous Land's End Hotel. The event, however, would be an awards ceremony, hosted by the John O'Groats to Land's End Company. This would be to officially acknowledge the First End-to-End wheelchair push for which I would be awarded the 'President's Trophy'. I looked forward to the ceremony, as this would include the privilege of a gastronomically delightful dinner and an overnight stay for Matron and me at the beautiful Cornish resort. In the meantime, there was another unusual wheelchair charity fundraising event that awaited me!

With just over four weeks to go, I returned to the Leasowe Lighthouse which my chair and I had previously ascended a couple of years earlier. This time, after again ascending to the top, I abseiled – in my chair – down the outside of the 135ft structure. This endeavour was a real 'tester'. It was with difficulty that I managed to control a persistent spin. This caused me to repeatedly crash into the wall of the lighthouse during my rapid descent. I also endured a somewhat heavy landing but my effort was totally worthwhile. I am more than a little proud to say that my eccentric effort helped raise over £5,000 for the Royal Institute for the Blind charity. Due to this endeavour being another 'first' I was interviewed again at length by

Swasie's 135ft abseil down Leasowe Lighthouse, Wirral.

the press. I took advantage of this by ensuring that my approaching Falklands push would be given as much publicity as possible. Consequently, as with previous activities, I started to receive donations for SAMA and Clatterbridge before I even left the United Kingdom.

As the time continually drifted by, my constant visits from Reg the Vicar continued. I owe a lot to this wonderful gentleman and I will never forget his relentless, caring and benevolent efforts to console both me and my daughter Jo. My ever vigilant GP Doctor Marion Smethurst made sure that she was fully aware of my health and welfare at all times by insisting I visit her regularly. She too is an absolutely priceless diamond. Her constant care and involvement does not know any bounds whatsoever. However, during my next visit to her after the lighthouse 'jaunt', the concerned doctor, fearing for my safety, didn't hesitate to chastise me for performing such a risky act. I reassured her that I was in control at all times during the, admittedly 'hairy', event. Nevertheless, as she looked at my grazed and cut hands and leg, it was plain by her expression I hadn't convinced her!

I continued giving my 'after dinner' talks as well as paying a further visit to the Lomax factory at Dundee. After this, Matron and I again travelled down to Bodmin where I gave another fundraising address. Prior to my departure for the South Atlantic, I had one more major 'appointment' to attend. This was a, very posh, 'Black Tie' dinner engagement where I dined in the company of some very high profile VIPs. The prestigious dinner was held at the extremely upmarket Burlington Hotel, Birmingham. I had the highly envious honour of being seated between two very pleasant and modest gentlemen. On my left was seated the ex-Governor of the Falklands (during the 1982 conflict) Sir Rex Hunt, and to my right sat the Lord Lieutenant of the Midlands, Robert 'call me Bob' Taylor. The dinner was in aid of SAMA 82 and a very pleasant evening was enjoyed by all who were present. Unfortunately, it had not been made clear that although Matron and I had been invited to stay at the hotel, it was only *me* that had been named to dine! Sadly, while *we* were all wining and dining in complete luxury, Matron slipped out for a cup of tea and a hamburger to satisfy her insatiable hunger! However, she joined the festivities after the dinner.

The following morning Matron and I were joined by Sir Rex at the breakfast table. This time, gone were all the fineries of formal attire and glittering gongs. The three of us sat and enjoyed our full English breakfast; Sir Rex and I were both unshaven and minus our ties. Sir Rex invited me to dispel with the 'Sir' and just refer to him as Rex. We exchanged cards with a view to subsequently keeping in touch, which we still do on occasions. What an extremely modest, courteous and friendly gentleman ex-Spitfire pilot Rex is. Although the cost of the tickets for the previous evening's SAMA 82 'bash' and subsequent overnight stay were expensive, such expense was well and truly justified. I had no qualms whatsoever and was more than happy to put my hand in my pocket and contribute to this extremely worthy cause. I was also proudly relishing the chance to enhance SAMA's coffers further by my forthcoming Falklands trip, which was now almost upon me.

On my return home I was interviewed the following day by the *Sunday People*. The paper subsequently published an illustrated full page feature regarding my fundraising endeavours which included the imminent Falklands push. Finally, and at long last, the big day dawned.

CHAPTER FOURTEEN

New Horizons

On a wet and very windy October Sunday morning, after consuming a hearty breakfast, I set about making a final check to ensure that I had packed everything I needed for my journey to the other end of the earth. Matron and I loaded the car with my luggage and my wheelchair. We also loaded a brand new, second wheelchair, donated by the generous Mr Wilmot of Lomax. This was for the King Edward VII hospital at Stanley, East Falkland. Prior to us setting off on our journey down to the Oxfordshire airbase, I received a telephone call from Denzil Connick to say that he too was en-route to see Richie and me off on our journey to the South Atlantic. Matron then drove us down to RAF Brize Norton where I met my firefighter and ex-Para pal Richie and his co ex-Para Denzil. The four of us sat in the lounge chatting about the forthcoming Falklands push as we awaited the arrival of our aircraft. Chris and Denzil remained with us until our boarding and travel formalities were concluded. During this time we all enjoyed the warm hospitality of Brize Norton, whose staff not only furnished us with copious amounts of tea but two of the bar staff, Stella and Sue, collected the sum of £90 for our coffers. Finally, it was time for us to make a move. Matron kissed Richie and me goodbye, and waved us both a cheery farewell before setting off on her long drive back home to Wirral.

Before boarding our aircraft, Richie and I were interviewed and photographed by the national and military press, and were then escorted out to make our way over to the waiting Tri Star. I 'negotiated' the steep steps up to the aircraft while Richie followed behind, ready to catch me! With everyone watching, I felt as though we were re-enacting the children's story of Jack and Jill went up the hill.....! More photographs were taken as we ascended the aircraft steps. On reaching the top, I turned to wave a final farewell to those below before entering the cavernous interior of the plane. The courteous RAF stewardess then kindly ushered Richie and me down the isle to our seats. In no time we were thundering down the runway and lifting up into the dark grey clouds before bursting through into bright sunlight as we ascended to 39,000 feet to begin our long, 8,000-mile flight South. We both dozed intermittently as well as enjoying the in-flight facilities and lavish gastronomical delights offered en-route. The attentive cabin staff ensured that our high standard of comfort was maintained throughout the whole of our journey.

Approximately eight hours after leaving a chilly, wet and windy Brize Norton, our giant of the skies, Tri Star ZD 592, landed at Ascension Island; a beautiful, tropical little paradise nestling 4,000 miles away in the warm turquoise waters of the mid Atlantic. Ascension is approximately halfway between the UK and the Falklands.

During the refuelling stop, Richie and I were given a brief look around nearby Georgetown, courtesy of Police Inspector Reg Williams and WPC Sandra Crowie of the British Saint Helena Police, who are responsible for policing Ascension. Although this is not the 'norm', Richie and I were privileged at being afforded the mini tour due to the unusual mission we were about to undertake down on the Falklands. Sadly, our extremely interesting but very brief tour was concluded and we were returned to our aircraft to resume our journey onward to the Falkland Islands. As we lifted off from the beautiful little utopian island, I vowed to return to Ascension one day; perhaps I would go with Matron.

During our long but comfortable flight, we enjoyed cuisine which was second to none and watched a couple of up to date films. The RAF went to great lengths to ensure that everyone on board wanted for nothing. The cabin crew were true professionals and absolutely first class. Finally, as we approached the Falklands, two Tornado jets took up station on each side of our aircraft to escort us for the last leg of our journey. At last, our long and tiring flight totalling over sixteen hours was concluded when we landed at Mount Pleasant airfield alongside the garrison on East Falkland. As we descended the steps from the aircraft, the caring and reliable crew were patiently waiting at the bottom with my chair. After entering the terminal building, recovering our luggage and passing through HM Customs, Richie and I were met by the Islands' acting Police Chief, Inspector Len McGill; a thorough gentleman of the highest order. We loaded our gear and the two chairs into the Police Landrover, then Chief McGill drove us to Stanley, the Islands' capital, 35 miles away. As the quaint, tin roofed town of Stanley boasts its very own Cathedral, Stanley is in fact a City. Darkness soon descended upon us and on our late evening arrival at Stanley, Chief McGill drove us straight to our new 'home'; a detached, hilltop bungalow overlooking twinkling lights of Stanley Harbour and the moonlit panorama of distant hills beyond. Our arrival was enthusiastically and warmly complete when we were greeted by two other extremely warm and hospitable hosts: Falkland's ex-Police Chief, and the Islands' SAMA representative Mr Terry Peck MBE and his charming wife Elly. What a fantastic couple they were. Each of these two wonderful people were 1982 decorated heroes in their own right, as were *many* of the courageous islanders during those dark, distant days of the conflict. After ensuring we were adequately fed and catered for, the couple left us to settle in, promising to return first thing in the morning. Due to the lengthy flight, it wasn't long before Richie and I made for our beds and crashed out. Tomorrow we would be making for distant Port San Carlos, the venue where we would begin the long, overland trek to retrace the same route taken by our heroic and victorious forces back in 1982.

After a good night's sleep I woke at 6.00am and pottered about getting my bits and bobs ready for the new day's activities and forthcoming adventure. As promised, Terry and Elly arrived to fuss and furnish the four of with a hearty breakfast. After we had all eaten, Elly drove Richie and me to the studios of 'Falklands Radio' in the heart of Stanley. There, we were interviewed live on air by the beautiful presenter Liz Elliot, wife of local Police Sergeant 'Jock' Elliot. Sergeant Elliot, was an ex-Gordon Highlander who had previously served on the Falklands. At the conclusion of our radio interview I was brimming with optimistic confidence and high morale, even though I didn't know what to expect. I looked forward eagerly to the start of my 72-mile (cross country) wheelchair 'Tab'. Richie too was delighted to be back among the very people he helped to liberate. Those same people didn't hesitate to elevate the veteran ex-Para to celebrity status. He was one of their true heroes who had come back to help them once again. My chest swelled with pride at such a wonderful reception we were receiving from everyone we met. In such company as Richie and Terry Peck I felt extremely humble. One pitch-black night during the 1982 conflict, Terry Peck fled into the mountains on a 'stolen' motor cycle to join forces and remain with the Paras. During that time Terry excelled by repeatedly risking his life to audaciously gain and photograph extremely valuable intelligence about enemy movements, which he then passed on to our forces. Due to Terry being a constant and extremely dangerous 'thorn in their side', the incandescent Argentine authorities put out a 'Wanted Dead or Alive' bounty on his head. For his brave and highly valuable assistance to the fighting British forces, Terry Peck was invested with a well deserved MBE from Her Majesty the Queen. There was no doubt about it; I was definitely rubbing shoulders with some people from the 'premier division'! I would strongly recommend the illustrated book named *Falkland Islanders at War*, as it includes Terry's contribution in the 1982 conflict.

After returning from the studios and after consuming yet another cuppa, Richie and I climbed aboard Terry's Landrover. The three of us then left Stanley en-route to far away Port San Carlos. During our long and bumpy ride, as Terry drove along he pointed out various points and venues of interest relating the conflict. Occasionally he would stop and we would be given the history of a battle here or a firefight there. We inspected a couple of downed 'Argie' aircraft, one being a helicopter. Terry gave us both a very interesting and educational 'Battle Tour' of the island as we headed on along the rough tracks. After hours of negotiating the rutted, hilly and sometimes boggy terrain across the country, we eventually arrived at Smylies Farm, Port San Carlos, the home of Jenny and Tony Anderson. Here, Richie and I would spend the night before starting in earnest the following day. The close and warm relationship between the Islanders was amazing. Everyone would help each other if and when needed without any hesitation, and without expecting anything in return. Jenny immediately set about furnishing Terry, Richie and me with a hot cup of tea. Within no time, a sumptuous dinner of mashed potatoes, green vegetables and layers of prime beef, all home grown, also appeared on the table. Jenny then instructed us all to tuck in to her wonderful and copious supply of delicious food. Not one of us was allowed to leave the table until all our plates were 'licked clean'! This typical example of Falklands' hospitality was truly overwhelming. The Anderson's modest home was immediately and unhesitatingly placed at Richie's and my disposal. If we wanted anything whatsoever, it would be ours for the asking. We were to find that such generous and deep benevolence was common throughout the whole of the Islands. Eventually, Terry was allowed to leave after clearing all that had been placed before him. Terry bade us all goodbye, informing us that he would return the following morning 'mob handed'! He would be accompanied by members of the Police and Falkland Islands' Defence Force, who would then escort us for some of the way.

After consuming more tea, and Richie enjoying a few beers with Tony, Jenny showed us to each of our rooms. Again, as per the previous night, once our heads hit the pillows, Richie and I immediately succumbed to the anaesthetic of heavy slumber.

The following morning I was woken by the sound of clattering dishes and cutlery. Richie then entered my room and ripped the warm blankets from my prone, naked body with terse instructions such as 'I say Swasie, you really *must* get up as your breakfast is ready!' – or something like that! A short time later, as promised, the 'cavalry' arrived in the form of Terry Peck in his Landrover, Len McGill and his Sergeant, Jonathan Butler, in *their* Police Landrover together with members of the Falkland Islands' Defence Force in *their* Landrover. What an extremely impressive sight to see! Richie turned to Terry and bantered, 'Well there's no chance of *another* invasion with this number Terry'! His comments brought laughter from all present. Jenny then added her gem by contributing, 'Bloody 'ell, I 'aven't seen this many troops since the invasion in '82.' However, all jokes aside, Richie and I were not only profusely grateful for such an enthusiastic and encouraging turnout, we were both so proud to be in the company of such great people.

The day's weather was cool and overcast with slight drizzle as we set off. Jenny gave Richie and I the added privilege of a kiss before we moved away from Smylies farm and on along the 'wheelchair unfriendly' track. Chief McGill and Terry Peck expressed their concern at the forthcoming, extremely steep gradient up and out of Port San Carlos. Chief McGill asked me how I wanted him and his men to assist me, or whether I would prefer one of the vehicles to tow me to the top. Richie quickly countered, 'Let the bugger manage by himself, he's big enough!' Chief McGill and Terry didn't know how to take this as they didn't think that the steep, muddy track up the hill could be negotiated unaided, especially in a wheelchair on casters. Indeed their concern was not without foundation, as I very soon found the going was very difficult. The muscles on my arms and shoulders felt as though they were going to burst with the exhaustive efforts of my input. The gradient was so steep in places that I turned around and *pulled* the wheels thinking it would be easier if I ascended in reverse. It wasn't! Many times those accompanying me pleaded to assist by pushing me. No way would

Inhospitable Falklands terrain.

I allow this. I turned to push forward and during the climb I fell out of my chair when it tipped over backwards. This was to be repeated many times during the 72 miles. Before those rushing to help me had chance to do so, Richie's dulcet, 'sympathetic and ever caring' rhetoric once again instructed, 'Get up you lazy bastard, you're not here to lie in the road resting'!

Richie's apparent lack of sympathy was part of our ongoing mutual banter. I knew very well that if I wanted his help it would be forthcoming in an instant. What everyone thought was a lack of sympathy from Richie was in fact a deliberate act of verbal inspiration! His 'unsympathetic' comments and innuendo were actually a tonic and a big encouragement to me. His constant brand of 'micky taking' was typical of Paras and Royal Marines and I loved every minute of it. I maintained my ongoing grunting and panting struggle until finally, I managed to reach what had seemed to be the hill's summit. My aching arms then propelled me over the brow for a further couple of hundred yards, enjoying the sheer luxury of a flat length of terrain. I stopped to take a much needed couple of minutes' respite to get my breath back. Chief McGill confirmed that everyone present (except Richie) whispered amongst themselves that they did not think I would get my chair out of Port San Carlos and to the top of that first hill. Before I was allowed to move on Richie, my complete mentor, thrust a bottle of water in my face insisting I consumed at least half of its contents. Only then did he allow me and our little posse to continue on through the mountains and over the heaths. Slowly but surely we managed to maintain our painful consumption of the miles as the day wore on. Apart from securing my welfare, Richie also performed his equally important duty of making sure that the whole of the trek was recorded on film for posterity. The pedantic Richie never failed to take pictures whenever he thought appropriate, He even photographed my various tumbles and falls, together with the resultant cuts and bruises they brought about. He had obviously received lessons from the equally 'hard' Matron back home! Due to these regular recordings of my various undertakings by those who accompany me, any doubts that could occur are eliminated by the illustrated proof the photographs bring about. This in turn hopefully guarantees that my charity bucket is enhanced as much as possible.

As we plodded and wheeled along I suddenly heard someone shouting. I saw a man standing near to what appeared to be a large hut and he was waving frantically to us. As we got nearer we realised he was inviting us all to join him. We made our way across the tough 'diddle dee' (a form of thick heather which bear red edible berries) to him and his 'hut'. As we approached, suddenly a large number of people disgorged themselves from the front door. The dozen or so men and women ran to Richie and me and smothered us both with hugs, welcoming us all to their meagre and humble abode. Their house was in fact two large converted ship's containers joined together. Richie and I were enthusiastically and unceremoniously dragged inside the 'house', and I was *still* sitting in my muddy chair! We were followed by our entourage and the rest of the resident occupying 'Hillbillies'! The cramped, bare-floored confines did not minimise the warm and generous hospitality so eagerly afforded to our little group.

Considering that money on the Islands was not exactly flowing, each individual member of the family gave willingly to ensure that our charity bucket received an extremely generous amount of cash. After consuming our tea and mutton sandwiches, we extracted ourselves from the generous family's cramped home and, after thanking them for their warm welcome and generous donations, we resumed our onward trek which would take us to Goose Green. This venue brought particularly vivid memories for Richie, as it was during the battle for Goose Green that Colonel H (VC) and Richie's pal Mark Holman-Smith were killed. After we stopped to lay a wreath (from Mark's devoted parents) at the Goose Green memorial, we enjoyed a cuppa with one of the local residents in their home nearby.

A couple of hours later, after pushing for an extremely exhaustive eight hours the day's activities eventually came to an end. Terry and the 'gang' left us to return home while Chief McGill transported Richie and me back to Jenny and Tony's farm. Once inside the warm confines of their home, Jenny ensured that I soon savoured the delights of a steaming hot bath, change of clothing then yet another hearty dinner of 'half a cow and a field full of vegetables'! After dinner Richie and I sat and enjoyed a very pleasant evening with our hosts, with each of us reminiscing about our individual past and pedigree and also the 'conflict'. We were also educated as to the future concerns of the islanders and what life was like on their remote South Atlantic Islands. Eventually, as all good things come to

Swasie salutes fallen Paras at Goose Green, East Falkland.

an end, Richie and I made for the welcome sanctuary of our beds to 'crash out' once again after a truly hard day.

The following morning, after another full English breakfast, Tony deposited Richie and me back where we finished the previous day's push. The two of us then pushed on across the inhospitable landscape towards the so far elusive and distant Stanley. Sometimes Richie and I would take a nap in a ditch or sheep sheering shed out of the persistent, chilling wind or rain. As the push progressed we were regularly monitored and accompanied by the police or members of the FIDF. Terry Peck would also accompany us and would drive his Landrover ahead and park it on the horizon waiting for us to reach it. The reason he did this was to give Richie and me an idea of the distance we were covering, as he always insisted that he parked his vehicle a mile away each time. However, we soon discovered that many times the distance was nearer two or more miles.

Consequently we referred Terry's distances as 'Im*Peck*able Miles'! Sometimes Terry and Richie would alternatively drive the Landrover on to the next Im*Peck*able mile point leaving the other to walk with me. The four days and three nights' push went well. During the distance covered we stopped at many places. At Teal Inlet we stopped at a little house where another charming hostess, Gloria Thorsen, greeted us warmly and invited us in to join her and her family for tea and scones. Gloria took the steaming kettle from her Rayburn cooker and immediately furnished us all with mugs of tea. Gloria held out a large spoon full of sugar and asked, 'Who takes sugar?' Her trembling hand scattered the sugar everywhere as she spoke and I replied, 'Everyone by the look of it Gloria!'

As we progressed, we were joined by islanders from near and far. A news cameraman Robin Fryatt, assisted by his wife Sylvia, filmed parts of my push as I struggled to propel my chair across the difficult terrain. We were later welcomed and given sanctuary at the isolated little Port Louis complex, where we were again luxuriously treated by Peter and Melanie Golding who also gave generously to our bucket. Although the push was to raise funds for SAMA, I also intended that a large donation would be made to 'my' cancer fund as Clatterbridge Oncology Unit treats patients from the Falkland Islands. After leaving Port Louis our little entourage was numerically increased when we were joined by Councillor Phil Miller and his charming wife Sheena. They had travelled many miles from Cape Dolphin specifically to accompany us for part of the trek.

One day, as Richie and I tabbed on alone, we stopped to spend an hour or so fishing for mullet using mutton tied on a length string as bait. We sat on rocks alongside the cold waters and, amazingly, we caught a number of very large fish. One fish dropped off my line and lay on the surface, I had no intention of losing it so I reached out to try and retrieve it. Forgetting that there was no leg on my right side, I fell headlong into the freezing water. Although Richie quickly helped to retrieve me from the 'oggin' he nevertheless fell about laughing hysterically! I shed my shorts, pants and vest and stood naked, shivering as I wrung them as dry as I could. Richie was beside himself giggling like a little schoolgirl! Eventually I was able to don my half dry clothes. This was just as well because a Landrover drove up and stopped alongside us. The driver was a woman! I asked the lady, Mrs Trudie McFee, another heroine of the 1982 conflict, if she would like some fish. Trudie gratefully accepted the mullet and donated generously to our bucket. This wonderful lady was to become another lifelong and dear friend.

As we neared the end of day three, having pushed 23 miles, Richie and I were again joined by our old pal Terry Peck. Terry stayed and escorted us the rest of the way to Estancia where we would conclude the day's push. Unknown to Richie and me, Terry had alerted our next overnight hosts of our impending arrival and as we came over the brow of the hill, we could see two people standing at the side of the track at Estancia Farm in the distance. As we reached the two, named Ailsa and Tony Heathman, they greeted us warmly. Terry, Richie and me were quickly ushered inside their neat little house. Within no time, Ailsa served us with a generous helping of mutton pie accompanied with the usual Falkland amount of home grown vegetables. After this we were shown to our rooms and then Richie thrust a telephone in my hand and said, 'It's for you, it's Matron!' I was delighted that Matron had succeeded in getting her long distance phone call through to me in the middle of nowhere! After concluding our call I was once again allowed the privilege of a long hot soak in the bath. As with everyone we had met during our stay on the island, the Heathmans made sure that Richie and I wanted for nothing. Like Terry Peck and Trudie McFee, the Heathmans too performed many extremely risky and heroic deeds during Argentine occupation of 1982.

At 7.30am the following morning, after an extremely beneficial and therapeutic overnight rest, I joined Richie at the breakfast table. Ailsa made sure we 'fuelled up' by serving us a lavish breakfast of wild Upland Goose eggs, penguin eggs, beans and home made bread and butter. Even the luxurious, world famous Dorchester

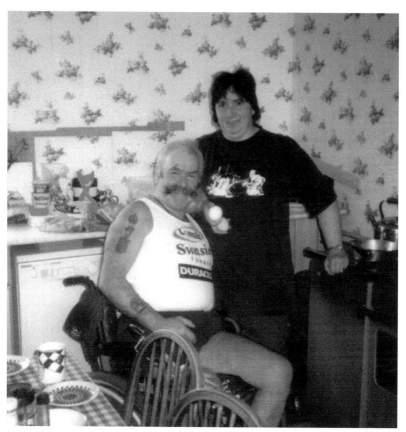

Swasie about to enjoy a penguin and wild goose egg breakfast.

could never match that! After finishing our breakfast we sat and awaited the arrival of our final day's escort, Police Chief Len McGill.

A short time later Chief McGill and his sergeant, Jonathan Butler arrived and we all set off on the last leg of our long overland journey to the island capital, Stanley. Again the push was hard, especially the slow crawl to the top of Estancia Mountain. There we were joined by a further contingent of people that included a reporter from the island newspaper *Penguin News*, members of the FIDR and the lovely lady interviewer, Liz, from Radio Falklands. The morning's push was also being filmed for TV World News by Robin Fryatt.

By the time I eventually reached the top of the mountain my hands were cut and bleeding, and to make my discomfort worse the heavens opened with a vengeance. I was soon soaked to the skin by the torrential downpour; however, my spirits were not in the least dampened. I knew that at long last our goal would be reached at the end of the day's trek. I was elated. The rain came down in sheets as we made our way past the minefields each side of the new Mount Pleasant to Stanley road. Suddenly, the rain stopped as quickly as it began. Then the sun emerged as we approached the capital. A number of motorists and a couple of coaches appeared. When they stopped, many of the passengers from the coaches and cars joined us to swell our ranks. Workmen at a nearby quarry complex came to hand us many generous cash donations and pose for pictures to be taken by their workmates and the press.

As our, by now very lengthy, procession arrived at the outskirts of Stanley, we were met by a fire engine and its crew, more police vehicles as well as a considerable number of Stanley residents, some with their dogs. At the 'Welcome to Stanley' sign we all stopped for a memorable photo shoot before descending the long hill onto the windy Stanley waterfront. Finally we arrived at the Stanley War memorial, as we had originally planned, on Saturday, 11th November 2000, where Richie and I were greeted warmly by His Excellency the Governor, Mr Donald Lamont. His Excellency shook my hand and congratulated me on successfully completing what he and most had considered to be a 'bridge too far'. After also offering his warm congratulations to Richie, we both laid a wreath at the Stanley Memorial. The Governor then formally invited Richie and I to dinner at Government House. What an accolade for the two of us to savour! Marje would be immensely proud of this latest achievement to raise much needed charity funds, an achievement *totally* inspired by her treasured memory. Richie and I were later afforded the additional honour of being invited to lead the official Armistice Day Parade through Stanley the following day, Sunday 12th November 2000. That was indeed the ultimate privilege.

On the day, Richie and I, fully 'booted and spurred' in our best 'BD' with highly polished 'Gongs' displayed, set off at the head of the long procession of troops. Following us, the band of Her Majesty's Royal Marines led the long, proud line of pristine uniforms. Fortunately the wet and windy start to the day had now changed to become dry with a slight breeze. This meant that everyone would remain looking smart in their finery instead of turning to sopping wet rags. Richie proudly donned his 'Red Beret', as did Terry Peck, who had been made an honorary member of the Parachute Regiment, and we led the large parade. This consisted of the military, cadets, police, fire, scouts and guides marching, with me wheeling, proudly to the War Memorial where the emotional Remembrance Day ceremony was held.

After His Excellency and Senior Officers of the Falklands Garrison laid their wreaths, the representatives of all of the Islands' authorities followed suit. Richie and I also laid wreaths we had brought from the UK. A Royal Navy warship lying at anchor in Stanley Harbour fired a final saluting salvo to conclude the very moving ceremonial proceedings. As the blue, billowing smoke from the ship's guns drifted slowly along the harbour front, the band struck up again and, to the beat of its drums, we resumed our march to attend a service at Stanley's impressive Cathedral, standing behind its four huge protective whale jawbones vertically pointing to the heavens.

That evening Richie, Terry Peck and I enjoyed a fantastic revelry at the nearby Malvina Hotel; the name has no bearing whatsoever to Argentina or the 1982 conflict. During the evening I was amazed to see how versatile many of the islanders were. Stanley Hospital's Medical Officer Dr Diggle, Police Chief McGill, Sergeant Elliot and his wife and His Excellency the Governor, each gave musical renditions and songs 'par excellence' to enhance the evening's entertainment. It was well after midnight before Richie and I eventually returned to our bungalow to 'hit the sack' after an absolutely wonderful and most memorable day. The following day

H.E. Governer, Swasie and Richard Helleur about to go on parade.

brought yet another little ceremony. Sergeant Elliot collected Richie and I and the new wheelchair – a gift from Lomax – then conveyed us to the King Edward VII Hospital at Stanley. On arrival we were greeted by Dr Diggle. A reporter and cameraman were also present as I formally presented the new wheelchair which had been sent down with us as a donation to the people of the Falkland Islands by Lomax of Dundee. After the little ceremony was concluded and photographed, the doctor and members of the hospital nursing staff conducted Richie and I on a tour of the hospital.

To put icing onto the day's 'cake' Richie and I, accompanied by Mr and Mrs Peck, attended a formal dinner hosted by His Excellency the Governor and his wife Lynda at Government House. This privilege too would remain a treasured memory of our Falklands endeavour. All too soon our wonderful South Atlantic adventure came to an end. My Falkland trip is an event that will remain vividly and indelibly printed in my memory forever. As with Ascension Island, I intended to return , perhaps to carry out another charity fundraising event.

After a sad, final round of visits to as many of our hosts as possible, courtesy of our chauffeur Terry Peck, Richie and I bade our extremely warm, hospitable and generous hosts a sad goodbye. We

Swasie presents Dr Diggle with a new Lomax wheelchair for King Edward VII Hospital, Stanley.

winged our way back to the cold, wet shores of England. As we left our aircraft at RAF Brize Norton, it seemed only a couple of hours since we were boarding our plane to set out on our most unusual endeavour. Due to our effort and the extreme generosity of those magnificent people of the distant South Atlantic islands, the coffers of SAMA 82 were increased by over £6,500. In the next few days, Richie would be resuming his duties as a firefighter back home in Bodmin as though he had never even been away. I too would be back home dreaming up and preparing for whatever my next fundraising venture would be.

Dinner at Government house.

CHAPTER FOURTEEN – NEW HORIZONS

In no time the Christmas period arrived again; a whole year seemed to have just evaporated as it had sped by. I *still* could not bring myself to invest in a Christmas tree or erect decorations in the house as my feelings regarding celebratory festivities remained non-existent. At 4.00am on a very frosty Christmas morning, accompanied by my ever faithful Alsatian dog Max, I pushed the five miles along the icy roads to my beloved wife's grave and sat with her for a while before returning home. I was surprised to see Matron up and about when I got back; she was 'patrolling' the lounge with the vacuum cleaner and busying herself with household chores. I was certainly lucky to have her looking after me as well as my ever-caring daughter Jo. Later, Matron left to have Christmas dinner with her family while Jo and I spent our day celebrating Christmas together. The Christmas period duly receded into the mists of time and lo and behold, we were now entering *another* new year.

I sat fantasising about the past couple of 'empty' but busy years and sincerely hoped that my fundraising would continue to be as successful. I now wondered what on earth this, the second year of the new century, would have in store for my future endeavours?

CHAPTER FIFTEEN

A Royal Invitation

Although now having moved on into the 21st century, I was still encountering all sorts of discrimination against the disabled fraternity. In this particular field, legislation has been introduced in the form of the 'Discrimination Against the Disabled Act' and is *slowly* bringing about a change. However, the creation of 'Disability Awareness' is without doubt, still in its infancy. More needs to be done, especially by the authorities, to bring this about.

As stated, every day, I either witness or experience ignorant behaviour in one form or another from people who seem totally devoid of courtesy and good manners, or are just selfishly oblivious to those they could quite easily assist in one way or another. On numerous occasions I have experienced scenarios where friends, and even relatives, are desperate to find a reason to eliminate giving me a lift in their car to a venue. They try to find excuses to save having to place my wheelchair into their car. This is not only extremely embarrassing but also deeply insulting and hurtful. I have spoken to a lot of people in a similar situation who confirm that they too have encountered similar behaviour from their so-called friends and relatives. Many times as I sit alongside Matron in a restaurant, a waiter will ask her, 'Does the gentleman have any 'special' dietary requirements?' The only way to combat this (apart from verbally biting such offenders' heads off) is for Matron and me to adapt to the situation when I'm tempted to act as though I'm not 'all there'! Many times however, Matron will retort curtly, 'Why don't you ask *him*? It's his *leg* that's gone not his *ears!*' A perfect example of this was when I attended an 'after dinner' engagement at one of Liverpool's most prestigious hotels to give an illustrated address to a 'black tie' audience. First, Matron and I had to negotiate wet concrete steps from the kerbside minus any offer of assistance from the Commissionaire. He stood and watched me struggle while Matron ascended carrying the cases containing my laptop and projector. Ahead of us was a revolving door. It was obvious that my chair would be unable to pass through this or the nearby side door, unless I was removed from the chair so that it could be folded and passed through. Finally, Matron had to take matters into her own hands and use her initiative. She put down her cases then unbolted the centre of the revolving doors and opened them out flat so that I could then pass through. Once inside, we witnessed a number of staff standing near the reception desk watching our every move! Not *one* came over to offer assistance. Matron then asked where we were to go to give our address to the formal meeting. We were told it was on the first floor, but the lift only started *from* that floor!

The two of us then had to negotiate, unaided, two flights of carpeted stairs to the first floor. I was absolutely 'delighted' at having to grunt and groan my sweaty way up on my bottom as I unceremoniously dragged my trusty chariot while everyone just stood about and gawped in silence. At the conclusion of the dinner, the whole operation was then conducted in reverse! I was incandescent with rage at such total inconsiderate conduct from the pathetic staff at such a prestigious and upmarket venue. As we were leaving the establishment, Matron could not resist the temptation to enlighten those present who could have been more helpful, including the open mouthed Commissionaire, as to their inconsiderate pedigree! Needless to say I would *never* allow myself to be placed in such an undignified predicament again. Also, I will not hesitate to inform the appropriate authorities and bring to their notice any flagrant disregard or lack of facilities for the disabled at such venues in future.

I continued giving my illustrated addresses to various schools, institutes and associations and yet again applied, for the third time, to take part in the London Marathon. This time, as I had already successfully completed a push across East Falkland as well as pushing from John O'Groats to Land's End, I pointed out that if I was refused entry again, I would seek redress through the courts via the Discrimination Against the Disabled legislation. After my two previous, unsuccessful attempts to gain entry into the event, I received what I considered to be a 'face saving' and audacious reply from the Marathon authorities. I was told that for the first time the London Marathon was considering allowing an NHS type wheelchair to take part in the forthcoming event, and asked if I would like to take part to see if this could be done. I welcomed the 'invitation' and, after paying my fee, my current application was accepted. Consequently, on the day of the run, I was allocated a place at the 'Blue' start. However, I was met on arrival by two stewards who informed me that Mr Storey had given specific instructions that I was to start at the back, *behind* the mass of fun runners! I was told to remain where I was and would be soon escorted to my allocated place where I would set off. I immediately vanished and threaded my chair to the front of the massive crowd of runners. I set off with the others without mishap and eventually covered the long and demanding 26-mile course. My little front casters finally rolled over the finishing line of the 2001 London Marathon (the first NHS wheelchair to do so) in the supersonic time of 7 hours 4 minutes and 59 seconds! I am immensely proud to have completed the event in my standard chair, and I hope my stubborn persistence will inspire others in a similar position to apply to take part in future London marathons. I have set a precedent which I hope will eliminate the chance of anyone else being prevented from taking part in such a high profile and world famous event. Thanks to my determined efforts to take part, my endeavour raised a lot of pennies for the Clatterbridge Cancer Fund. As expected, the completion of the marathon in such a basic conveyance brought a tremendous amount of publicity, to the absolute delight of Lomax. They were ecstatic that one of their products had, for the first time, entered and completed

Swasie and his pal, Sub Officer Peter Dan, complete the London Marathon.

the much revered event. This of course enhanced the advertising capabilities of their extremely reliable and robust product considerably, even though it hadn't been constructed for such use! I too was more than overjoyed at the thought of giving the previously obstructive and doubting 'Jobsworths' one in the eye by my ultimate success.

Throughout the months I also continued my regular visits to my GP. The regular 'bucket revenue' I generated was enhanced by once again completing the fifteen-mile Wirral Coastal Walk. This was followed two weeks later by a parachute jump from 15,000ft at Hinton-in-the-Hedges to raise more funds for SAMA 82. On landing, I had the honour of being presented with my honorary 'Para' wings by Major General Julian Thompson, the Commander of 3 Commando Brigade during the Falklands conflict of 1982. At this time I decided to contact both the Falkland and Ascension authorities with a view to once again completing a charity fundraising event on each island. I contacted the two authorities and was absolutely delighted to receive a positive response from both. I intended to push the 35 miles from Mount Pleasant to Stanley to raise funds for a Falklands charity, and also wanted to attempt the annual 'Dew Pond Run' on Ascension Island. Both of my requests were endorsed with enthusiastic encouragement. There was another reason for my return visit to East Falkland; I was to present a trophy I had designed and had specially made to be given each year to the winner of the 'Pembroke Half Marathon' which was an annual Falklands event. Now, we would all have to get cracking once again and sort out the logistics for such endeavours.

The day after the parachute event at Hinton I received an official looking letter through the post. The letter was from Buckingham Palace inviting Matron and I to a garden party at the Palace on 11th July! We were gobsmacked! Both of us were overwhelmed at the thought of meeting the Queen and couldn't wait for one of the most important days of our lives to arrive. Among the tasks I would be performing would be the purchase of 'Top Hat and Tails' while

Matron went looking for a new hat and party frock! Hardly having had time to recover our breath after receiving our Palace invitation, we then travelled 300 miles down to Land's End for the earlier planned End-to-End Awards ceremony at the Land's End Hotel. Matron and I dined at the very upmarket hotel and after the meal the prestigious ceremony took place. I was awarded the 'President's Trophy' for having completed the John O'Groats to Land's End push in 'the most unusual' conveyance. I decided I would proudly put it on display when I returned home. After our posh overnight stay, we returned home having completed over a 600-mile round trip. I was now ready for my *next* event, which would be my second 'Bikeathon'. With my friends Mr and Mrs Creek, I again completed the 26-mile course (and *again* came in last) to add to the much deserving coffers of the Leukaemia Research Fund in memory of Malcom and Gillian Creeks' daughter Alison. This year too seemed to be flying by, during which I attended another Mobility Road show with my generous sponsors Lomax.

At long last the big day arrived for Matron and I to attend the Buckingham Palace garden party. Looking resplendent in her party frock and her large pale blue 'bin lid' hat, Matron and I (a grey top hatted wheelchair 'penguin') were met by a Royal Protection Squad police colleague outside the Palace gates. Constable (now Sergeant) Adrian Hey escorted Matron and I through the palace grounds to the beautifully manicured rear lawns. During an extremely pleasant afternoon we had tea and sandwiches, and had the ultimate and unbelievable honour of meeting Her Majesty the Queen, as well as Prince Phillip and also Prince Charles. We spoke to each separately as they regally meandered among their guests. I just could not believe that I was actually here! Matron too was equally overwhelmed by the extremely high honour of our day's visit. 'Lady Christine' and I could not believe we had been elevated to such high, social status!

Nine days later, my Palace visit still foremost in my mind, I set out to push my chair from the 'Cotswold Care Hospice' in Stroud, Gloucester, to far away Dudestacht, a little town near to what was

Swasie and Matron arrive for the Palace garden party.

once the East German border. The push of over 500 miles was to raise funds in England for the hospice and the Fire Services National Benevolent Fund and, when over into Germany, my push would raise funds for the German Disabled Charity Fund, the Libenshilfre. At the conclusion of the usual press and photo shoot, I had the privilege of being seen off from Stroud by the town's Lady Mayoress, before being escorted through the town by a fire engine, Mr Wilmot and my Lomax backup driver Grant Gardner. The fire engine stayed with us for most of the journey to Cirencester. After losing my red escort I pushed on for the rest of the day's journey with Grant at a discreet distance behind. Eventually we stopped at the retained fire station for our overnight stay, on the lecture room floor, at the picturesque little town of Burford. My seven-day push down through England went smoothly and numerous donations were received en-route. The overnight comforts afforded to Grant and me were well catered for by the kind and extremely hospitable firefighters of Slade, Aylesbury, Hitchin, Bishop's Stortford, Colchester, Clacton and Harwich fire stations. Due to the extreme generosity of the people en route which included all the firefighters, the cash in my charity bucket was well into four figures. Matron drove down to Clacton for a brief visit before Grant and I eventually crossed the channel. While she was there, she and I both helped with a charity car wash at Clacton Fire Station to 'top up' the bucket!

As I pushed the last few miles to the ferry in the pouring rain, Grant and I were accompanied and escorted by a Harwich fire engine. After completing formalities, Grant and I boarded our DFDS Seaways ship, the 'Admiral of Scandinavia' and settled down for a pleasant overnight voyage to Hamburg. On the day following our arrival in Germany, I set off from Brake to start my long, 14-day push to Dudestacht. Two days later, my Lomax backup driver changed. I lost Grant who was then replaced by Art Sangster; both of these men are certainly jewels in the Lomax crown. My push was physically hard but the German people were extremely kind and hospitable, and my bucket quickly filled with donations wherever my travels took me. Art and I were interviewed by TV and press at Bremerhaven and other places along the way, and were generously hosted and escorted by the German *Polizei* (police) for much of the route. We spent our overnight stays with local residents, a priest and at fire houses as well as a couple of hotels. The German sense of humour sometimes did not match that of my own, which brings a particular incident to my memory. After an overnight stay with the priest, Art and I were sat at the Holy Father's breakfast table consuming our boiled egg and toast. When my plate became devoid of toast, I innocently asked the Father, 'Where's the Holy Ghost Father?' as I often use rhyming slang. In my unthinking naivety I was seriously asking, 'Where is the toast?' Taking me seriously the Father looked to the ceiling and spread his arms wide and replied in perfect English, 'Swasie my son, he is everywhere!' Instantly realising my faux paux I agreed wholeheartedly by saying, 'Yes, you can actually *feel* his presence can't you Father?' Art looked at me and smiled wryly, after he had winced at my unintended, but nevertheless thoughtless and ill-mannered, blunder.

As we slowly proceeded through the beautiful German countryside I was fascinated by the number of large, wooden, ornamental windmills that adorned many of the neat little gardens I passed. When I spotted the place where they were made I couldn't resist purchasing one as a souvenir. My new acquisition was then loaded into our van which was carried for the duration, until it was eventually sited in my garden on my subsequent return home.

Swasie with Anton the Priest at breakfast.

I experienced many adventures as I pushed my chair across Germany when I would pick and consume apples from roadside trees and eat ears of ripe corn which I gathered from the golden fields. Sometimes my backup was unable to follow me when I meandered along narrow tracks or through forests. During these times I would navigate via a small map on my lap or follow the fast flowing River Wesser.

Eventually I completed the long hard journey, which was a resounding and fundraising success. I was given a *polizei* escort into the little walled town of Dudestacht, and was amazed at the tumultuous welcome I was afforded by a very large crowd who had gathered to welcome our little entourage. I had the honour of being invited onto a large stage to be formally greeted by the town's Burgomaster (Mayor), other local dignitaries and a German MP. I gave an amplified address to the people thanking them profusely for their warm welcome and generous German hospitality. My speech was translated by a member of my Lomax team, Shona Spence, who was responsible for coordinating the German side of the push.

On my jubilant return to England, as well as resuming my talks at various venues, I set about preparing for the next major endeavours which were now looming on the horizon. This time, when I visited Ascension and the Falklands, I would be accompanied by my big brother Tom. After my summer and autumn activities, there was one more event to complete before November arrived when I would return to the South Atlantic.

On Sunday 30th September 2001, I travelled down to Nottingham to take part in the 26-mile 'Robin Hood' Marathon. My effort would raise more funds for the Fire Brigades 'Ben Fund'. As soon as this was over, in no time the day arrived when Matron drove Tom and I down to RAF Brize Norton to begin winging our way to distant lands. We enjoyed our pleasant trip down to the Falklands, which included a brief refuelling stop at Ascension where we would spend a few days on our return trip. On arrival at Mount Pleasant we were met by my old Police Chief pal Len McGill. This time I was armed with my treasured innovative gift to the Falklands;

The town of Dudestacht greeting Swasie at the end of his 500-mile push from England.

it was the gleaming, new, most impressive silver and mahogany based 'Marjorie Turner Memorial Trophy', which I would present to His Excellency the Governor. The trophy would be awarded to each year's 'Pembroke Half Marathon' winner. We loaded out bags and my chair into the spacious police Landrover and headed off to our 'base' at Hillside army barracks, Stanley. Our host was the C.O. Major Jamie Haywood of the Scots Guards, who later chastised me for calling his Labrador dog Sam; 'It's not Sam, it's *Samantha*'! he corrected me curtly. We also met 'Ogre', the awesome six-foot six Regimental Sergeant Major, a really great man. Len and Terry Peck described my previous Falkland exploit in detail to Tom, and later we were driven over my old route for him to see for himself. My brother was truly mesmerised on seeing what his kid brother had accomplished over such barren and mountainous terrain. We called at the various places I had previously visited and I introduced Tom to my many friends on the island. We enjoyed the warm hospitality of Ailsa and Tony Heathman, Trudy McFee and Tony and Jenny Anderson at Port San Carlos.

On completion of the arduous 35-mile push from Mount Pleasant to Stanley, over £700 was raised for the Falklands King Edward VII hospital at Stanley. The cash was formally presented to Doctor Diggle at the hospital later. After completing the push from Mount Pleasant to Stanley, we were met and welcomed into town by His Excellency the Governor, Mr Donald Lamont, who again afforded me the privilege of being invited to dinner with Tom at Government House. There we would join the Falkland's garrison Commander as well as Terry and Ally Peck and other high-ranking dignitaries. Tom, like me, was very impressed at being at being invited to such a formal evening with the Falklands' 'Powers that be'! During dinner Tom sat between two ladies, one of whom was Mrs Peck. I asked His Excellency if it would be okay for Tom, him and I to be photographed. 'Certainly' the Governor replied, and invited Tom to leave his seat and stand between him and me at the top of the table. Tom rose and, turning to the other lady next to him, handed her his camera. Tom went to great lengths telling the lady how to take pictures and gave explicit instructions as to how she should direct the camera and press the shutter. The lady acknowledged that she had 'basically grasped the situation' and would try to do as Tom asked. After a couple of pictures were taken, Tom resumed his seat and continued to enjoy the Government House cuisine. As dinner progressed Tom engaged the lady with idle chit chat and casually asked her, 'What do you do for a living then?' The lady turned to my brother, smiled and casually replied, 'I'm Head of the Antarctic Expedition Photography Unit'! The following evening, the Malvina Hotel was the venue of another important ceremony when it hosted the trophy presentation. The hotel was filled to capacity when I formally handed the Marjorie Turner trophy to His Excellency during, what was for me, an extremely moving and emotional ceremony. I think this also had a similar affect on my brother.

On Sunday 11th November, I was once again given the honour and privilege of leading the Remembrance Day parade to Christ Church Cathedral, Stanley for the dedication service. After this we

The 'Marjorie Turner' trophy.

moved on to lay wreaths at the 'Cross of Sacrifice' to conclude the day's ceremony. Before Tom and I left East Falkland to round off our memorable stay, we enjoyed a further day's therapeutic outing when we were driven out for a most enjoyable picnic near the scenic settlement of Port Louis by Trudie McFee and a couple of her friends.

The next day Tom and I were driven to Mount Pleasant. We bid our hosts a sad farewell then boarded our RAF TriStar for the long trip North to Ascension Island. As we 'rotated' and rose from the runway we were again joined by two escorting Tornados. Looking down from the crystal clear sky we could see the little houses and the cathedral far below on the Stanley waterfront. The flight to Ascension was consumed by us watching films, enjoying the RAF cuisine and the occasional 'cat nap'. Finally, we dropped down onto the tropical Island and were met once again by our Ascension host, Police Inspector Reg Williams. Following the usual arrival formalities Tom and I were taken to our basic but comfortable accommodation at Hayes House, opposite the Island's administration building. It certainly is *no* exaggeration to describe the Island as 'paradise'; life there is so laid back, and there is no crime whatsoever. The Island's inhabitants are mainly from the equally beautiful island of Saint Helena (who are referred to as 'Saints') and they are some of the most friendly, courteous and considerate people I have ever met. As well as its wonderful people, the Island also boasts beautiful scenery, exotic birds and wildlife, while warm, transparent tropical waters of a turquoise ocean gently kiss its scenic coastline. There was much for Tom and I to explore while we were here. I intended to raise funds for the Island's Scouts and Guides during my stay by completing the infamous 'Dew Pond Run'! This is a very popular annual event on Ascension. It involves a seven-mile 'run' from the sea at Georgetown along through the village of Two Boats, then ascending to the steep 2,817ft summit of Green Mountain, an extinct volcano. Upon entering the Dew Pond Run my application was met with a similar, but extremely polite, reaction of disbelief that

I had previously experienced from the London Marathon. The difference here was that although nobody thought I *would* reach the top of the mountain, my application was not refused; it was encouraged! Inspector Williams took Tom and I to meet His Honour the Administrator (the Island's Governor) Mr Geoffrey Fairhurst and his charming wife Wendy. As on East Falkland, our wonderful hosts ensured that our stay would be one to remember.

The day arrived for the Dew Pond Run to take place and I joined the large number of runners at the water's edge at Georgetown. Tradition demands that each of the runners must first dip their hands in the sea before setting off, then, at the conclusion of the run at the top of Green mountain, the performance is repeated by again dipping their hands into the Dew Pond at its summit. There was not one person who believed I would get my chair as far as Green Mountain, let alone negotiate the jungle foliage to reach its summit. I think my brother too was definitely a 'Doubting Thomas' on this occasion!

After setting off I was very soon left way behind. However, there were two kind young Tornado pilots who volunteered to stay with me and slowly we made progress along the Island's 'highways'. After pushing up through the villages of Travellers Hill and Two Boats the going got tougher as the gradients became extremely steep. Many times I turned my chair round and pulled myself backwards; I had to keep doing this to make progress up the ascending tracks and paths. Eventually the paths vanished and gave way to grass which became longer and more dense. I pushed and forced my way through bamboo, banana trees and mud. Many times I was passed by people, who, having reached the top, were now descending back homeward. I was frequently (and annoyingly) informed that there was no way I would get to the summit. My struggles went on and I relentlessly pulled, pushed, crawled and clawed my way upwards. The only concession I allowed myself was the two pilots parting the bamboo canes as I forced myself through the undergrowth. I dragged my chair up the last (almost vertical) hundred feet and burst out into

Green Mountain, 2,817ft, Ascension Island.

daylight. Unbelievably, and against all odds, I finally did reach the summit of Green Mountain and immediately complied with tradition by plunging my sweaty, mud-caked, cut and scratched hands into the cool water of the mountain top pond. My trusty wheelchair and I had actually completed the Ascension Island Dew Pond Run! The two pilots and I were greeted enthusiastically by the half dozen event officials who couldn't believe the achievement they had witnessed. My sweat soaked, muddy vest was duly stamped with the event's official 'summit' stamp bearing the words, 'ASCENSION ISLAND–GREEN MOUNTAIN 2,817ft The Peak and Dew Pond' which signified confirmation of the truly awesome ascent, an endeavour I would *never* forget. After savouring the 'stratospherical' delights of my high incline, I duly returned down the mountain. However, this time, those accompanying me insisted on attaching a rope to my chair to eliminate the temptation of fate and prevent further undue risks. They didn't want to see me vanish into the distance at a rapid rate of knots, 'bottom over chest' as the saying goes! Eventually we reached my brother who had remained with some officials and their vehicles when I made my final assault to the summit. After further hugs, hand shakes and jubilant celebrations, I quaffed numerous bottles of water to restore my fluid loss. Tom and I were then driven in an RAF Police

Swasie at 2,000ft, Green Mountain, his starting point seven miles away in the distance, left.

Landrover back to our accommodation at Hayes House where I washed and changed into clean dry clothing. A generous collection was later forthcoming when I gave a talk at the community hall in Georgetown. I donated all the money I had raised via my day's activities to the Ascension Island Scouts and Guides Association, a *very* worthy island cause.

Following the successful completion of the Dew Pond Run, Tom and I received an invitation from His Honour Geoffrey Fairhurst to join him and his wife Wendy for dinner at Government House, the official Governor's residence. The next day, we couldn't believe it when the Administrator's car, with the British pennant flying proudly from its bonnet, arrived at Hayes House with Geoffrey himself as our personal chauffeur behind the wheel!

Geoffrey first drove us on a 'magical' mystery tour around parts of the Island as we headed up towards Green Mountain. Our journey took us through the tropical vegetation, past the deep chasm of the notorious Devil's Ashpit, hidden amongst the lush greenery of palms and bamboo. Geoffrey pointed out to us the many places of interest that abound on the island. Finally we arrived at our prestigious destination, 'The Residency'. We turned into the impressive tree-lined driveway and, beneath an overhead canopy of trees, rolled down towards the house. We passed through another gateway and I saw the Union flag fluttering proudly above the neatly manicured 'baize' front lawn. We were greeted by Geoffrey's charming wife Wendy who ushered us through the house to the equally pedantically tended lawns at the rear. Later, dinner was served and we dined on the patio, waited on by the warm, friendly Residency staff. We sat and admired the stunning view of Georgetown and its adjoining dazzling white sandy beaches far below. The elevated Government House commanded a panoramic view which included the whole of the maritime approaches to the Island and the lengthy, two-mile landing strip at Wideawake Airfield. After our extremely pleasant meal, Wendy proudly gave Tom and I a conducted tour of the Residency after which we enjoyed drinks and canapés out on the terrace under the hot tropical sun. Tom stood fascinated and enthralled from his lofty perch, and took numerous photographs of the various stunning views. He then 'spied' on the distant, bustling Georgetown far below in the distance through a pair of powerful binoculars. If there was a better place on earth to be, I certainly could not think of one at that moment.

During the following days before our return home to 'Blighty', Tom and I enjoyed the company of some off-duty aircrew during their rest periods on the Island. Also, Wendy, being the island's museum curator, gave my brother and I a detailed tour of the small Georgetown museum, explaining in detail some of the ancient and extremely interesting items on display. Soon, our most exotic and wonderful stay came to an end and it was time to return home. As we left the island utopia, I now definitely intended to return with Matron one day so that she too could experience the magnificent

Swasie's brother Tom with his Honour and wife at 'The Residency'.

tropical paradise that is Ascension Island. All too soon Tom and I, each sporting a deep tropical tan, arrived back at Brize Norton on a cold and wet late November morning. There we were greeted by the ever dependable Matron and transported back home to the wet and chilly Wirral. My extremely busy year was brought to a close after illustrated talks to the young ladies of Pensby Girls' school. As the year 2002 was approaching, I wondered what it would bring.

CHAPTER SIXTEEN

More Mega Mileage

My first 'After Dinner' talk of 2002 was an address to the Wallasey Lions on 7th January. Although the Lions are well known for their benevolence towards worthy charities, I was bowled over at the conclusion of my talk when I was handed a cheque for £1,000! To put it mildly, I was *more* than surprised at the amount of money they deemed my effort was worth! The cheque was made out to my Clatterbridge Cancer Research Fund. My talks to various organisations continued and I was also busy arranging to push 286 miles from the White House, Washington DC to the Pentagon and then on to Ground Zero, New York. I had been in contact with a member of the Washington S.W.A.T. Team, Officer Wendell Cunningham and his senior officers, to seek their assistance in the venture.

I intended to raise money for the traumatised Emergency Services victims of the atrocious terrorist attack on the American World Trade Centre on 11th September 2001. A lot of hard work ensued between me and the US Authorities, which included the White House, Washington Police and Fire Chiefs as well as their colleagues along the entire route. My intentions were given wide publicity by the media, not least by Shirley Chisnall the editor of the UK's *Police News*, *Fire News* and *NHS News*. Due to Shirley's elaborate coverage of my intentions, she was immediately inundated with an avalanche of volunteers from all three services throughout the whole of the United Kingdom. Everyone wanted to assist their American brothers and sisters in their time of need by accompanying me and raising much needed financial assistance.

It took a lot of planning to bring the event to fruition, but eventually my efforts bore fruit. Thanks to the kind permission of the individual Police and Fire Chiefs, I was able to select a team to accompany me on my fundraising 'pilgrimage' to America. My team consisted of Constables Andy Davies and Alan Landrum of the Merseyside Police, firefighters David Balmer and John Cash also from Merseyside, and Bodmin firefighter Nigel Honey, followed by Mr Graham Farrell and Mr Ron Schank, a US immigrant and now a Merseyside Paramedic. Once formed, our motley crew immediately set about starting to fill our US bucket by completing a local twelve-mile walk along the roads of Wirral. We were accompanied by a police Landrover and a fire engine which drew the attention of the generous public. This readily donated to our worthy and very high profile cause. We also raised large amounts of cash as we stood outside local supermarkets with the blessing and encouragement of their managers. As well as customers, the staff at these establishments, which included Sainsbury's and Asda, also gave generously. A local Wirral pub, The Clipper (now The Sandbrook) held a charity evening solely to raise funds for our forthcoming endeavour. The patrons' generous donations on the night raised the level of our bucket enormously. To enhance our efforts further, I was invited to attend the parlours of the Mayor of Wirral and the Lord Mayor of Liverpool. Each of the ambassadorial dignitaries, as well as handing me a cash donation, also gave me a gift to take to the Mayor of New York. The airlines too assisted our efforts considerably when Virgin and BMI allowed us all our return travel at half price.

On our arrival in Washington it is safe to say that we were treated like royalty. We were invited as guests of honour to various establishments who *all* donated heavily. A press and photo shoot was held at the office of the Washington Police Chief, followed by a similar visit to the Washington Fire Chief before we moved on to the FBI Headquarters. Later, in the evening I went on a 'routine' police helicopter patrol over the capital city. The following day we were all wined and dined at the British Embassy.

Although it had previously been intended that we would have an audience with President Bush, unfortunately his extremely tight Middle East schedule prevented this. However, we were still seen off from the White House by the civic dignitaries and senior officers of the Washington establishment. Outside, at the front of the most impressive building were parked numerous fire trucks, ambulances, police cars, state trooper's cruisers and limousines together with their accompanying crews and occupants. We were given a warm send off speech by the Police Chief and Fire Chief who stood behind a large wooden lectern to give their amplified rhetorical gratitude for what we were doing. Huge crowds had gathered to witness the impressive spectacle as we were bid a fond farewell. Sirens wailed as our long procession moved off through the streets of the Capital on our 286-mile trek towards the distant city of New York. Bystanders were fascinated at the sight of a vest and shorts clad man in a wheelchair heading two British 'bobbies' and their firemen colleagues through their crowded streets. The money flowed into our buckets right from the start and our 'motorcade' was nearly a quarter of a mile in length.

The second day saw us make through Baltimore. The town has a very poor quarter and in parts the anti-police feeling blatantly shows. However, amazingly the very same people, being aware of our fundraising trek did not hesitate to swell our coffers. Small children, tramps and many who were obviously not financially endowed, contributed enthusiastically. Paper money fluttered down and coins were thrown to us from windows as we passed by. It was a humbling experience to be on the receiving end of such sacrificial generosity. We were visited and accompanied by television crews from Fox TV and other news channels, and motorists, lorry drivers, hotels, and all who were near enough donated as we made our way along. As soon as our long procession stopped for refreshments, we were immediately swamped by hordes of people. This was brilliant as not only were we making friends with our American hosts everywhere we went, but also our buckets were filled to the brim. As we headed

Swasie and his British colleagues during the lengthy 286-mile push.

the large contingent of police, fire and state troopers and their vehicles, Jonny Cash proudly held aloft the British Union flag while our resident 'Yank' Ron Schank did likewise with 'Old Glory'! By the end of each day we had filled a large glass demijohn with cash. We had many adventures en route and met numerous VIPs as we passed through towns and states. Our party was sometimes split overnight when we stayed at firehouses (not fire stations), but most of the time we spent our nocturnal periods together.

We were filmed almost every day by the various TV news channels as well as being interviewed by the press. The American hospitality was at all times truly overwhelming. Finally our long and arduous trek drew to a close and we eventually reached the well-known Brooklyn Bridge. As we neared the end of our mammoth walk I was greeted and interviewed by a BBC television camera crew and their lady presenter. Our interview was subsequently beamed across to Great Britain. We were also interviewed and filmed by American TV networks as we pushed over the mighty span across the Hudson River. My 'gang' and I then had the honour of being greeted by the British Ambassador who was patiently waiting for us at the end of the bridge. Again our British party was mobbed by well wishers and donors. We were then escorted by the Ambassador, TV, press and a large crowd as we headed to the smoking remains of what was once the thriving World Trade Centre. Sirens wailed and car horns blared adding to the chaos our procession was causing. We had now, at long last, reached the final stage of our long and weary journey of homage; Ground Zero. My British team and I were then given the VIP privilege of being taken inside the strictly enforced cordon, directly to the centre of operations. Here, at the large 'shrine' to the glorious fallen, we read cards and letters addressed 'to Daddy', or 'My Darling Husband' and equally tear jerking notes and messages to those lost in the atrocity. Every one of my party unhesitatingly wrote out and left our own individual messages to our fallen comrades; one or two of my pals also left items of their uniforms. One red eyed rescue worker, a fireman covered in dirt and grime, came to me in tears and threw his arms around me. He sobbed words of thanks to us Brits, calling us 'their heroes'. I quickly and emotionally corrected him by informing him that it was *he* and his colleagues who were *our* heroes!

The scene at Ground Zero was then made even worse when another body was found almost underneath us. The deceased was a fireman. He was quickly but solemnly removed with the utmost dignity, and as his shrouded body was taken away on a stretcher, all present stood (I sat) to attention and saluted. A senior police officer scolded a television cameraman, asking him to give me and my party some space and privacy as it was clear we were overwhelmed by what

Ground Zero.

we were witnessing. Even though every single one of us Brits had *all* experienced dealing with death, tragedy, burned bodies and the like, every one of us were nevertheless overwhelmed with humility at being in such courageous company as they performed their ongoing, unenviable and gruesome tasks.

Later, we dined with the rescue workers in their large tented complex at the scene. Their work was ongoing and relentless as they searched the massive ruins for human remains among the twisted steel, shards of glass and overhanging masonry. They had been at this with hardly a break since the world-shattering incident happened, some short twenty weeks before.

As in Washington, our New York hosts feted us enthusiastically and we were given a tour of the 'Big Apple' where we met 'everyone who was anyone'! Due to the enthusiastic benevolence of the generous people on *both sides* of 'The Pond', over $38,000 was raised for our 9/11 push. I was afforded a personal privilege when I was invited by Mrs Donna Hickey, widow of the late 9/11 fire hero Captain Brian Hickey, to join her and her family for dinner at her detached home out in the New York suburbs. There, she asked if I would wear her late husband's MIA (Missing in Action) bracelet. I thanked her generously and assured her it would grace my wrist from then on. This was, to me, the ultimate honour from someone who was still deeply traumatised at her own inconsolable loss, but who could still find time to acknowledge the efforts of others. Such consideration surely amplifies and emphasises the critique I so often level at those who behave to the contrary. My proud but sad team and I returned home to resume our own domesticity after our most unique achievement. The whole scenario was once again pedantically featured, with dramatic pictures, via Mrs Chisnall's skilled, journalistic quill in all three of her widely read newspapers.

During this, the year 2002, being the year of Her Majesty Queen Elizabeth's Golden Jubilee, I wanted to do something special. I wanted to complete something as a form of loyal celebration, but at the same time, maintain my fundraising capability. As I regularly raise money for another charity close to my heart, the Fire Services National Benevolent Fund – who have the privilege of Her Majesty being their patron – an idea was born that would bring about my next fundraising exploit! As well as continuing with my talks to maintain my regular cash contributions to my charities, I set about once again contacting the various fire brigades between my home in Wirral and London. My intention was to leave Wallasey Town Hall and push the 210 miles to Buckingham Palace with (hopefully) congratulatory messages for the Queen from Mayors and civic dignitaries en-route. My idea and requests for assistance were met with enthusiastic encouragement from all whose help I sought.

My push would also be to raise funds for the 'Ben Fund' as I made my way down the country to the Metropolis. I decided to take a copy of the book *Wheelchair Pilot* as a gift to the Queen. Finally, all the arrangements were completed and the audacious idea was ready to be put into practice.

On Monday 20th May 2002, I joined the Mayor and Mayoress of Wirral in their parlour at Wallasey Town Hall. They had kindly invited me to join them for morning coffee prior to my departure. Also present were the Lord Mayor of Liverpool, Mr and Mrs Wilmot representing Lomax, my daughter Jo and my brother Tom. The press were in attendance to record the unusual and memorable occasion for posterity. As I was cheered away by the many well wishers who had gathered to witness my departure, I was escorted by a Wallasey fire engine with Jonny Cash and Dave Balmer (of the US 9/11 push) among its crew. Bringing up the rear was my ever faithful Lomax backup van driven by my 'mentor' Mike Townsend. My first overnight stop was at Chester fire station and as I neared the old Roman city I contacted the city's Lord Mayor who kindly invited me to attend his Mayoral Parlour when I reached the City. On my arrival I was kindly furnished with a welcome cup of coffee and as I admired the lavish furnishings of his room, His Worship gave me a sealed envelope containing a message of congratulations for Her Majesty, as well as giving me a generous donation for the 'Ben Fund'. At the conclusion of my visit I made for the nearby fire station where I would spend the night. During my first night's stay at Chester the city was battered by heavy winds and rain. Thankfully this had abated by the time I set off the following morning and clear skies and a warm sun replaced the previously inclement weather. There were some 'naughty' hills as I made my way south with a brigade escort for the first three miles. The day's push was long and demanding and seven hours later I concluded the second day's push at Shrewsbury. After setting off the next day, although I had a head wind, so far my trek had gone well. We stopped for a bacon butty and a mug of tea outside RAF Cosford. A short time later

I resumed my push and after a couple of miles had passed beneath my casters, I was intercepted by the Lady Mayor of Newport who stopped us at the roadside. The kind lady, wearing her gold chain of office, handed me a letter for Her Majesty as well as a large donation for my bucket. A few miles further along the road a fire engine met us and provided an escort to Wolverhampton, my next overnight stay. During that evening I was interviewed by Pebble Mill Television.

The following day, after breakfast, I met the Mayor of Wolverhampton and again received a letter and kind donation as we were being photographed alongside a fire engine by the local press. I then set off with my fire engine escort for the first three miles, then we stopped at Stourbridge for another press call. Our journey then continued on, now minus my fire escort, towards my next distant overnight port of call at Redditch. As we neared the town we were met by the brigade and again escorted to our destination. As well as having a high profile escort, the fire and police vehicles always ensured the generation of interest and this of course brought about continual donations from the public. The days (and miles) went by and my push maintained a steady flow of cash for my bucket. I eventually reached another night's abode at Hemel Hempstead Fire Station. The next day after yet another press and photo shoot, my station 'colleagues' escorted me with their machine as I made my way out of town. We stopped at a large Sainsbury's store where we were given numerous donations by the customers as well as the benevolent manager and his staff, who also furnished us all with a tray of cold drinks. After eventually losing my escort I continued on until I was later met by a fire engine from Paddington, my last overnight stay before reaching the Palace. For the whole of my journey down to 'the Smoke' I had been inundated with generous offerings from 'Joe Public'. I also received many congratulatory messages for Her Majesty from the Mayors of each town I passed through. During my overnight stay at Paddington Fire Station the telephone never stopped ringing; the local press and radio were continually seeking to update their bulletins as to my progress. The whole enterprise was a massive and most successful PR exercise for the police and fire services, to which I am permanently indebted. Although the 'Ben Fund' would receive the financial result of my effort, I unhesitatingly acknowledge that without the assistance of my Emergency Services 'brothers and sisters', my ongoing efforts would not achieve the magnificent results they had so far accomplished.

After a pleasant night's slumber I washed and tidied myself up before joining the night watch for breakfast before they went off duty. However, as we were about to consume our gastronomical delights, the 'bells went down' (the station's alarms sounded) sending the crews out to an incident. It was 10.00am before we finally set off for the Palace, and this time I was escorted by the day shift crew. A uniformed police constable kindly walked alongside me to guide me through the unfamiliar labyrinth of London's streets. My two escorts, Lomax and the Paddington fire crew, remained behind and eventually I reached the Mall.

As I pushed along towards my final destination which was now looming in front of me, I couldn't believe it when I was then joined by the Household Cavalry and their accompanying mounted police officers. I arrived at the Palace with the Cavalry, the Mounted Police, fire engine and my trusty Lomax backup man, Mike. What a spectacle! The tourists snapped away with their cameras and as we arrived at the Palace gates, we were met by officers of the Royal Protection Squad who were awaiting our arrival. Coincidentally one of the officers, Constable Caruthers, is the son of my ex-Superintendent during my own police service. I was escorted into the Palace grounds and once inside I stopped by one of the scarlet coated Coldstream Guardsmen. I apologised to him and explained that I would be brief while Mike took a picture of us both as I sat alongside him. Although he never flinched, he muttered out of the corner of his mouth while staring straight ahead, 'I know you're Scouse, *I'm* from Liverpool too!' I quickly replied, 'Oh no, it looks like I'm going to finish up on bricks then?' Still not batting an eyelid but undoubtedly appreciating my Merseyside wit, the Guardsman muttered, 'Piss of yer cheeky bastard!'

I was taken inside the Palace where I handed all the letters and cards I had received, together with my book *Wheelchair Pilot* to one of Her Majesty's aides. Although I didn't see the Queen I did see Prince Charles who was about to conduct an investiture.

The push raised over £6,400 for the Fire Services National Benevolent Fund and during my lengthy trek I met and made many new friends. After returning to Paddington Fire Station to wash and change, my driver and I joined the firefighters for a hearty lunch before I was returned home to Wirral later that evening. The following morning I was out early to go and visit Marje, and later that day I attended an official Plaque Dedication ceremony, where I had the honour of opening a new library garden at Wallasey. The library's front wall accommodated a large, engraved brass plaque bearing my name, to permanently commemorate the formal occasion.

Some time earlier I had been invited down to Lympstone in Devon to give an illustrated talk of my 'physically demanding challenges' (as they put it) to injured Royal Marine recruits. I am more than happy to say that the senior officers at the establishment deemed my renditions a 'morale boosting' success. Due to this, I was asked to attend again and give a further address to other young Marines who had suffered injuries during their gruelling Commando training. Although I deeply appreciated such an honour and eagerly jumped at the chance to return, I nevertheless decided that it would be more pertinent if I were to undergo similar gruelling activities as the young recruits. I reasoned that if I too were to complete long distance marches and endurance courses, then I could 'look them in the eye' and we would all be 'singing from the same hymn sheet'! I voiced these sentiments to a courteous and extremely interested Sergeant Major Gill at Lympstone, who, although somewhat apprehensive at first, saw immense possibilities *if* my idea could be realised. Thankfully my second talk was deemed as

Sgt. Major Gill RM.

successful as the first, and I was also given the go ahead to accompany
the Royal Marines on a 30-mile 'yomp'. The subsequent event not
only boosted the morale of those I later addressed in the Falkland
Hall lecture theatre, but I also (unexpectedly) received more than
a generous donation for my cancer fund from the Lympstone
Sergeants' Mess. This endeavour brought about my fiercely loyal and
dedicated involvement with Her Majesty's Royal Marines at their
Commando Training centre in glorious Devon. I have now become
deeply involved with 'Hunter Company' at Lympstone; 'Hunter'
is the injured Marines' recovery unit, which is a 'company' where
those who sustain injuries during training receive top of the range

medical attention in various forms. After this they are usually able to move on and undergo intensive physiotherapy and therapeutic physical training in the gym, culminating in cross country 'yomps' and lengthy roadwork. This is where I join them on their '30 milers' and early morning speed marches. I have completed numerous Commando Endurance courses and abseils in my wheelchair and was eventually awarded my honoury, coveted, 'Green Lid'. I am *extremely* proud of this, the ultimate of awards and I am equally proud of being part of the elite , the 'Bootnecks' of Hunter Company at Lympstone! My involvement is such that I now attend Lympstone approximately every three months as part of their 'Hunter' company's rehabilitation programme. By the end of August my chair's milometer showed I had completed a total of 25,000 miles.

My heavy itinerary continued with talks which now included giving addresses to public libraries and hospital lecture theatres. Also, my GP continued with her monitoring 'vigil' as to my progress. As the year passed my daily early morning visits to Marje were occasionally interrupted by trips to Lympstone and Dundee. The hot summer months passed and the month of October arrived. On the 25th of that month, Matron drove me and a firefighter pal, Peter Dan (who walked part of the End-to-End with me) to Gretna Green where we met a contingent of Royal Marines. After enjoying a hot lunch we all set off for the far away Scottish highlands where we would be ascending the infamous Ben Nevis to raise money for charity. As we travelled towards Fort Augustus, where we would stay overnight at the village fire station, we stopped at Ann Matterson's stone cottage on the outskirts of Glencoe. Yet again the most hospitable lady fed and watered us all before we resumed to our ultimate destination.

The following morning, after a cold night on the fire station floor, we all made to Fort William Police Station. There, our Fort Augustus Fire Brigade host Dave arranged our breakfast and left a radio to enable contact to be maintained later while we were on the mountain. We were then visited by the local press, who followed us to

Swasie and team at the Commando Memorial prior to the ascent of Ben Nevis.

the Commando Memorial at Spean Bridge near the base of Ben Nevis. After we were all interviewed and photographs were taken, we set off to commence our all-out 'assault' on the mountain. The climb was excruciatingly difficult and at one stage my wheelchair fell over 100feet down the mountain, I 'baled out' and fell only twenty feet! The chair was subsequently retrieved (undamaged!) by Colour Sergeant Somerton-Rees who then kindly repatriated us both to resume our ascent. Unbelievably, we managed to reach as far as the reservoir, but here I met a three-foot wall of snow which prevented further wheelchair progress. A couple of the lads stayed with me while other members of our team went on to within 300 yards of the

Ben Nevis ascent cuppa.

summit. Here, they were advised by Mountain Rescue that due to adverse weather conditions it would be unwise to continue. Although the final ascent was well within the capabilities the Royal Marines, in the interests of safety they returned to me and we concluded our day's climb. We made our descent down to Matron, who was patiently waiting in her warm car at the mountain's base. The day's enterprise, however, was deemed a success and much money was raised.

The following morning, Matron, Pete, Dan and I bid our hosts and Royal Marine pals farewell and drove down through the 'kilted' gates of Scotland into England and returned to Wirral. Winter was upon us again and I was only too soon pushing along the frosty or sleet covered roads as I maintained my punishing, daily routine. In no time at all another (depressive) Christmas had passed and we were now entering the year 2003!

CHAPTER SEVENTEEN

Return to Paradise

After consulting the authorities with a view to completing another fundraising endeavour, we made arrangements for what would be another very challenging push. This would be an 84-mile cross terrain push from Fox Bay to Port Howard on West Falkland to raise money for the 'Stephen Jaffray' memorial fund. Matron and I saved hard for the trip and in the first weeks of January, I would now fulfil my vow to return to the South Atlantic with her where she would be able to savour the utopian delights of the islands and their people. We would stop off at Ascension on our return trip from Mount Pleasant. Even before I left my home for Brize Norton I had already received a generous donation for my bucket. My coal merchant, Mr Harry Taylor (H & M Taylor of Heswall, Wirral) handed me £50 as he delivered coal to my address the day before my departure. As the staff at RAF Brize Norton already knew me, they too expressed their benevolence by handing Matron and I donations on learning the reason for my current trip. I received further cash and cheques during our flight as well as on our subsequent arrival at Mount Pleasant, East Falkland.

Once again, my Falklands 'best' pal Len McGill met us and conveyed us straight to Estancia farm where we were greeted warmly by my previous hosts Ailsa and Tony Heathman – and their new pet lamb, Andre. After I introduced Matron, Ailsa showed her to 'our' room and after further informal chit chat, Len left us to it and returned to his home. Soon we were all sitting down to roast Upland goose and Estancia vegetables, after which Matron insisted on washing the dishes and pans, much to the delight of Ailsa.

Acting Police Chief Len McGill RFIP.

The next few days were busy for the Heathmans, sheering their massive flock of sheep before grading and packing the hundreds of fleeces. Matron and I helped in the sheds gathering the wool and placing it in sacks. Matron also assisted further by doing chores around the house for Ailsa, running the vacuum cleaner over the floors and bringing in peat for the ever hungry stove. Two days later I was interviewed on air by Liz Elliot at Falklands Radio after which Matron and I wandered around the shops on the Stanley waterfront before our return to Estancia. The next day we were invited to the Officers' mess at Mount Pleasant for me to give a talk. Our pleasant hosts plied us with generous amount of G and Ts (in Matron's case) and soft drinks for me. After a tour of the Garrison by our courteous host Squadron Leader David Freak (a real officer and a gentleman), we were returned to Estancia once again, interrupting our trip by calling for coffee with His Excellency the Governor at Government House. Matron was really moving up in the world! During the following couple of days, Matron and I were taken on a full tour of East Falkland by Len which included stops at Goose Green and Teal Inlet where Matron met Gloria the sugar sprayer! Once again I had the utmost pleasure of meeting old friends and introduced an impressed and extremely fascinated Matron to my previous hosts. Our visit was reported via an illustrated feature in the *Penguin News*, which, as usual, brought about numerous donations!

On a windy Sunday morning, Len McGill took Matron and I to Mount Pleasant where we boarded a helicopter bound for West Falkland. On reaching the island we were met by Falklands veteran, ex-Royal Navy pilot Roger Edwards, who would host our stay on West Falkland. As we made our way from the helicopter the rain started to pour down in 'stair rods'; we were soaked before we could manage to get inside Roger's Landrover. A short time later, after a short half-mile drive to Roger's house, we were soon washed, changed and sitting at the table enjoying a delightful dinner. We had roast duck with all the trimmings with Roger and his charming wife Norma who are both members of the Falkland Islands government. Fully refreshed after our most enjoyable dinner, Roger and Norma later took Matron and I to the Fox Bay Social Club. This is a large ship's container which boasts a bar and some tables and was next door to the local supermarket (another container). We all enjoyed a convivial evening during which all present donated to my bucket. I had now received well over £400 since leaving the UK. At the end of a most enjoyable evening, our hosts escorted us back to their large, comfortable house overlooking Fox Bay.

The following morning, Monday 20th January, after a full English breakfast I set off on my long push to distant Port Howard. The weather was atrocious with high winds and heavy rain. Roger and Matron followed me as they sat in the warm, dry confines of Roger's Landrover. After five long and strenuous hours of negotiating muddy tracks, fields and steep hills the day's push concluded with the completion of 51 miles. Our stopping point was at a desolate farm called Little Chartres, way out in the middle of nowhere. The kindly farmer and his wife furnished us all with hot mugs of tea and cakes. After a quick rub down and change of vest, Roger returned us to the haven of his home at Fox Bay.

The following day we resumed our journey to Port Howard which was now 32 miles away. The weather was kind at first as I started to push across the tracks and tufted grass away from Little

Swasie's Island friends.

Chartres. However, things changed dramatically! The rains came with a vengeance, accompanied by a bitterly cold wind. In no time at all I was cold and soaking wet. I tried to increase my speed to generate heat but to no avail. I could hear Roger's Landrover squelching through the mud and grass. I spotted a large, grey triangle with its apex pointing to the rain-sodden heavens as I struggled relentlessly on up a gruelling soggy hill of peat and puddles. When I neared the triangle I identified it as a delta winged Argentine Mirage Fighter, which Roger informed me had been shot down by a Royal Navy Harrier during the 1982 conflict. At this stage I stopped for a hot drink from Roger's flask. I was absolutely soaked and freezing cold. The rain cut across in sheets driven by the strong wind. Roger was worried and asked if I wanted to call it a day. I refused and stubbornly carried on with my push. A couple of times when my wheels sank into the peat I fell out of my chair and into the wet bog. Matron wound her window down (two or three inches!) and shouted to see if I was okay. I rose from the soaking, dark brown peat and said something like, 'Yes I'm alright dear, wind your window up or you'll get wet!'

After another five long, arduous and very slow hours pushing, I finally reached the muddy track leading past beautiful little houses and entered Port Howard. The first thing to greet me was a horse who stood across my path looking at me, wondering what the hell he was seeing. I patiently muttered something like 'Excuse me Neddy' as I dragged my sodden frame and mud-caked wheelchair past the fourteen hands, white-haired equine obstruction. A lady came out of a house and sloshed through the mud to hand me a ten-pound note. I thanked her for her generous donation and then Matron (bravely) alighted from the Landrover into the downpour and threw a kagool over my head; good thinking Tonto! As I moved on Roger dove in front to guide me to the warm sanctuary of the Port Howard Lodge, the local hotel half a mile further on. I couldn't believe that I was there at last and about to enjoy the luxuries of hot food and drink. The first thing I sought on entering the building was a hot bath; first to thaw me out, and secondly to wash away the copious amount of mud and dark brown peat stains from my body. In no time one of the staff had filled a large bath with hot soapy water and Matron removed my wet clothes and helped me into the soothing water. Almost immediately the bath's clean liquid contents clouded to the colour of treacle. Matron scrubbed me clean then left me to savour the delightfully relaxing and therapeutic soak. Fully warm, dry and attired in clean clothing I returned to join the others in the kitchen. I hungrily scoffed a number of freshly made Cornish pasties straight from the oven and washed them down with mugs of hot, sweet tea.

Eventually we left our charming hosts at the Lodge and as the rain had stopped, I accompanied Matron to the nearby jetty and we watched the porpoises leaping out of the waters as they showed us their aquatic skills. At times like this, it is easy to forget the discomforts I had experienced only a short time earlier. Matron snapped away enthusiastically, not wishing to miss such a wonderful display put on by Mother Nature. Unknown to me Matron had been continually ensuring a pictorial record was maintained throughout the whole of my push.

Finally, the day's fascinating activities at Port Howard came to an end. We all climbed into Roger's Landrover to be driven along the long, bumpy tracks and fields back to Port Howard. During our return trip Matron took pictures of the downed Mirage Fighter and Roger very nearly did a 'barrel roll' with the Landrover when we slid down a muddy hill sideways. This had definitely been a very eventful day and an extremely hard push but I was exceedingly proud. I had now successfully completed long distance pushes across both Falkland Islands to put yet another feather into my Marje's inspirationalcap. By the time we left Port Howard our cash coffers had reached the sum of £900! After returning to spend our last night at Roger and Norma's house we returned to Mount Pleasant the following morning. After further donations from residents on East Island, the sum rose to £1,000 which I formally handed to the late Stephen Jaffray's sister Lisa at Stanley Police Station during a formal

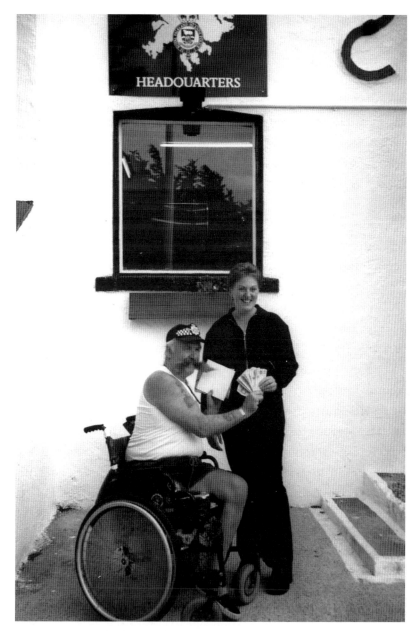

Swasie presents donations to Lisa Jaffray at Stanley Police Headquarters.

presentation ceremony. This was attended by the *Penguin News* and Radio Falklands.

Our stay on the Islands drew to a close and Matron and I were soon on our way to the hot sunny climes of Ascension. We were accommodated at Hayes House where brother Tom and I had stayed during our previous trip to the Island. Police Inspector Reg Williams took Matron and I to Government House where we were formally introduced to the Island's new Administrator (Governor), His Honour Mr Andrew Kettlewell. Our visit was featured in the Ascension newspaper, *The Islander*. The kind police chief later gave Matron and I a tour of the Island where Matron performed her regular routine of photographing everything worthy of recording. I certainly consider the standard of Matron's photography to be of professional quality. Her Ascension photographs of beautiful, exotic birds and panoramic seascapes are excellent, and even include nocturnal scenes of giant turtles laying their eggs in the sands of Clarence Bay. We swam in the local pool and lazed on the beaches during our exploratory stay, and I gave an informal talk to the Administrator and local residents at the Obsidian Hotel in Georgetown. After the talk, a pint glass was handed round which was filled with cash. The donated sum of £47 went to the Islands' Scouts and Guides. All too soon our exotic Island stay came to an end and we returned home to chilly England blissfully endowed with permanent, wonderful memories of our fantastic visit.

Now life was back to normal, I resumed my routine of daily pushes, talks and preparing for yet another series of fundraising events to furnish my worthy causes. As well as my passion for generating funds for charity, I was always on the lookout for ways of improving the 'lot' of those who were physically handicapped in one way or another. I thought about ways to improve various venues to make them 'wheelchair friendly', especially accessibility to places of recreation and country footpaths. I came up with an idea that could enable me to do both! I decided to push my chair 127 miles along the towpath of the Leeds to Liverpool canal. The push would be to raise funds for the Fire Services National Benevolent Fund and a donation to Clatterbridge, but also I would check the wheelchair accessibility of the whole route. On learning of my intention my kindly next door neighbour, Mr Andy Jones volunteered to accompany me on the lengthy week-long trek. The push would start from Leeds on Tuesday 25th March. As always, I enlisted the aid of the fire brigades en route, who enthusiastically offered me their assistance by providing overnight accommodation and meals. My old pal Peter Dan, a Merseyside Sub Officer drove Andy and me to Leeds where we stayed overnight at the town's fire station.

After breakfast the following morning, Andy and I were accompanied to the canal by a fire crew where photographs were taken by the brigade photographer. I had an altercation with a car park 'Jobsworth' who insisted on the crew purchasing a ticket to park on the (empty) parking area. After advising him to call at the 'Foreign Office' forthwith, I pointed out that the fire engine was there for publicity purposes and I pretended to take his picture with my camera. 'What yer takin' me picture for?' asked the council moron. I told him his picture would be in the forthcoming 'Jobsworth Times' and the man immediately changed his tune. Brushing his food engrained lapels and adjusting his grubby baseball cap, he asked when the magazine was out and I told him, 'every Friday'. He was delighted and told me he would make sure his wife and the whole of his family availed themselves with copies from his local newsagent. The fire crew were beside themselves as they stifled their grins.

At the conclusion of our 'photoshoot', Andy and I bade our brigade hosts farewell and set off for far away Liverpool. At first the push went well but very soon the concrete paving flags gave way to narrow mud tracks and grass. Further along there were bridges which were not easy to cross, especially those which had steps. I concede that these were not impossible to negotiate if the person in the wheelchair was being pushed by another person. However, as the push progressed things became more difficult when nettles and foliage went right to the water's edge. In other places there was no path at all. Andy and I were intercepted by Radio Leeds and interviewed over a cup of coffee at the Waterside Restaurant whose manageress handed us a twenty-pound note for our charity bucket. On seeing this the rest of her customers followed suit. We resumed our push £48 better off than we were before our cuppa. A couple of miles further along we were met by a fire crew from Keighley. Two of the crew walked with Andy and I along the bank while their fire engine rolled along the road nearby. We were escorted to Keighley Fire Station for our night's stay.

Our trek resumed the following morning as we made our way out into the isolation of the countryside. The only company we had were rooks in the nearby trees as we slogged on. The going got really tough as again, nettles and bushes caused me to force my way through and suffer cuts, scratches and stings. I was attacked by a ferocious and very territorial swan who didn't want me near his missus and kids!

Later still, I tried to push my chair along a narrow stretch of the bank but failed and fell headlong into the canal with my chair. That really made my day! Although Andy assisted me out of the water, like Richie on the Falklands, he couldn't resist falling about in hysterical laughter. Further along we stopped at a moored canal boat where the kindly 'mariners' gave us a generous donation as well as a cup of hot tea and sandwiches. Greatly refreshed we moved on and as we neared civilisation the donations started to flow. Many had heard the radio coverage earlier in the day. At the conclusion of the day's push at Skipton, Andy and I made for our overnight accommodation, the Hanover International Hotel. After a wash and change, members of the town's (retained) fire crew took us to a pub for a traditional 'Pie an' Peas' meal, courtesy of the management, who also donated to our bucket. The food was first class and after an evening with the pub's guests, Andy and I retired to our hotel to 'crash out'. Our bucket was now a lot heavier thanks to the people of Skipton.

Our push continued on the following day and we passed through Oswaldtwistle and on to Blackburn. Although the donations were many, and extremely generous, I needed to draw the attention of the various local authorities regarding disabled accessibility to their canal banks and towpaths. Many areas were causing me concern as there were high, locked gates and stiles and the paths were far too narrow for wheelchairs. I contacted British Waterways at their head office near Chorley and spoke to Mr Richard Byles. He listened sympathetically to my critique and courteously invited me to join him for coffee the following morning, so that I could air my sentiments further. As arranged, the next day I called to his canal side

Canal side obstacle.

office. Mr Byles listened intently to all I had to say and promised that my comments would be duly passed on to the appropriate quarter. In fairness, it must be pointed out that since my meeting with Mr Byles, I am aware that things have improved and the authorities are definitely doing their best to better things for the disabled fraternity. A lot of the gates and stiles have now been replaced by tubular steel 'A frames'. These are brilliant as they admit wheelchairs and infants' push chairs but they prevent cyclists, motor cyclists and horses from passing through.

Eventually the long push was completed and Andy and I were met by the Lord Mayor of Liverpool. In total we had raised the astronomical amount of over £2,000 for the worthy causes. Five days later, I met my friend Nigel Honey, the Bodmin firefighter who had accompanied me on the US 9/11 push. Our meeting was at Manchester Airport prior to our flight to Las Vegas. The purpose of this journey was to complete a fundraising push across the notorious and forbidding 'Death Valley' to raise money for an American cancer charity in Nevada. I had arranged with a fellow member of the International Police Association, ex-Police Chief Tom Savage, (who also suffers from cancer) for Nigel and me to complete the 108-mile push for a charity of his choice. Tom and I had worked hard to bring about this fundraising endeavour and on our arrival at Las Vegas airport, Nigel and I were met and taken to Tom's home on the outskirts of the famous desert city. After meeting Tom's wife Jean we each became 'engaged in combat' with a large American T-bone steak. The steaks were not only big, they were massive; the only things missing were the horns! Nigel and I were worried each may take a week to consume! The Americans certainly know how to eat. At least it would fortify me for what lay ahead!

Las Vegas is a truly fascinating place and is without doubt another hot and sunny paradise. The whole city is contained in a vast, desert 'bowl'; yet another 'jewel in the American crown'! During the day the hustle and bustle is just like that of any other busy town. However, at night the whole town erupts into a blaze of light.

Viva Las Vegas.

The world famous 'Strip' is a cascade of neon lights; pulsating, flashing figures and massive pictures invite all to the various establishments. Arcades are abound with loud music and there is a general carnival atmosphere. I was amazed to find that the town was already aware of its wheelchair visitor and the reason for my presence.

During the days before the push began, Tom took Nigel and I to meet the Police and Fire Chiefs who then courteously gave us a conducted tour of their departments. We visited numerous places of interest which included the homes of film stars. We even called at the impressive residence of Arnold Schwarzenegger and took pictures of his massive fortress-like home. Most of all we enjoyed our nocturnal visits to the Strip and the many vividly illuminated hotels and casino establishments. As I meandered along one evening, I was approached by a 'woman' who informed me she had heard about my forthcoming push across Death Valley. The 'lady' was virtually chatting me up! As I had spent some time in the Vice Squad back home, it didn't take rocket science for me to recognise 'her' as a transvestite. Maybe anyone who was naïve, or had not been around as much as I have, could well be taken in; however, I wasn't. I thanked the transvestite for her interest and verbally dispatched her forthwith! Nigel and Tom congratulated me on my having 'tapped off' with a 'lady boy'!

The following day started in earnest. We packed our bags and my chair into the large RV (recreational vehicle) which had been donated to Tom for the duration of our push by Sahara RVs of Las Vegas. Before setting off for Death Valley we called to thank the kindly proprietor and as we did so, the manager from Chick's Autos, next door came to us and gave us $100 for our bucket. Grateful formalities concluded, we set off on our long, hot drive to Death Valley. Our four-hour journey took us through Clark County, then Nye County before we reached Inyo County. Here we met Park Ranger Miss Nancy Wizner and Sheriff Bill Lutz. Bill would guide and additionally escort Nigel and I during my lengthy push through and across the hot barren wastes of the desert. After the searing heat of the day and the tiring drive, I enjoyed a good night's sleep at the Furnace Creek Hotel before leaving to start my push from Badwater the following morning. Even though we moved off immediately after breakfast, the sun was already beating down relentlessly. I pushed alongside Nigel on the endless desert strip of road. Soon my tyres were hot to the touch due to the extremely high temperatures (110°C in the shade!) and the sweat literally rolled off me in constant drips. Tom would drive his RV ahead and stop to wait for Nigel and I at strategic points every few miles with copious amounts of water. Sheriff Lutz would bring up the rear in his big police cruiser.

Las Vegas 'Ladyboy'!

Occasionally, motorists (when we saw them) would stop to give generously until we eventually moved 'off road' along tracks.

After eight long hours of almost non-stop pushing, Nigel and I concluded our hot day's trek. Tom transported Nigel and a soaking wet 'wheelchair pilot' back to the sheer luxury of the air conditioning at our Furnace Creek Hotel. After dinner that evening I presented Sheriff Lutz with a Merseyside Police helmet, a gift from Merseyside Chief Constable Mr Norman Bettison QPM (now a Sir). Sheriff Lutz was absolutely delighted with such a unique and very rare item of uniform, as anything like this from 'lil' ole' England is very much appreciated and sought after in the United States.

The next morning we plodded on from where we finished the previous day. The desert was baking hot and I encountered my first 'rattler'. I was negotiating some loose rock and kicked a stone away from one of my front casters and it crashed into a nearby little clump of shrub. I heard the immediately identifiable, rapid 'ticaticaticatica…' sound of an obviously angry rattlesnake which must have been disturbed by my unintended pot shot into the undergrowth. Nigel kept a beady eye on things as I manoeuvred my awkward chariot well away from the dangerous serpent at an extremely rapid rate of knots! Although we had been warned by Sheriff Lutz and Tom to keep a wary eye open for these venomous little demons, seeing one in the flesh so close was an experience that Nigel and I would never forget. From then on I treated every bush, clump of grass or shrub with suspicion. I had to reverse over more stones that were too big for my casters to negotiate, as well as soft sand and in doing so a scorpion suddenly darted out from his subterranean lair and scattered off to seek shade in a rockery elsewhere. Just to add to the toxic cocktail that prevailed in the arid environment I was struggling through, Sheriff Lutz also warned Nigel and I that the area housed equally harmful and nasty little creatures such as tarantulas and the infamous Black Widow spider! Needless to say I was absolutely 'delighted' to be in such wonderful, friendly company!

During our laborious crossing of the salt wastes Nigel busied himself 'playing Matron' by photographing the dramas we encountered in the wilderness. I saw various little bouquets of beautiful brightly coloured desert flowers that enhanced the hot environment, but I had been told it was a heinous offence to even think of picking any of them. Likewise it was an equally serious offence to remove a stone or piece of rock. This legislation was strictly enforced. Once back onto hard standing with Sheriff Lutz behind me, I whispered to Nigel, 'Hey Nige, watch this!' I finished drinking the contents of a plastic water bottle then tossed the bottle onto the ground. Tom couldn't believe what he had just witnessed and Sheriff Lutz nearly suffered a miscarriage! He dived out of his police cruiser and screamed at me to pick it up or 'He would bloody well shoot me'! When they realised it was another example of British humour, the two Americans rocked with hilarity at my audacity in front of authority. This amusing little episode brought the day's 23-mile trek to a close. I must admit, I had been very naughty earlier when Nigel and I were alone. Unknown to the Sheriff, I did pick a flower which I hid until I placed it into my diary and pressed it onto the day's entry page, where it remains to this day.

The following day's push took me to Stove Pipe Wells; an old Wild Western style pioneer settlement. It had a spinning wind generator, a solitary old fashioned, hand cranked petrol pump and a little store that sold provisions, guns and ammunition as well as a variety of handcrafted souvenirs. An almost antique fire truck was parked at the dusty roadside; its bright red paint now turned to a matt light brown due to years of exposure to the relentless desert sun. Nigel instantly asked me to take some pictures of him alongside the unique fire engine. Although we were way out in the middle of nowhere, there were a few motorists in their gas guzzling 4 x 4s and some wealthy tourists. I enjoyed the luxury of quaffing some iced tea and Gatorade to restock my fluid drained body. Everyone about the little 'oasis' gave benevolently and we received many donations from those we met and talked to. I have always found Americans to be extremely generous people. They were truly fascinated and extremely impressed at what we were undertaking for a US cancer charity.

Before we moved on I bought a couple of (genuine) souvenirs which included two glass paperweights; one housed a scorpion and the other, a tarantula. The former graces my desk and the latter lives in Matron's office. At the end of the day's push we were all invited to Park Ranger Nancy Wizner's house on the edge of Death Valley for a T-bone 'barbie'. What a great evening we had. Again, the steaks were the size of a scale map of South America! The amount of steak I was being fed over in the grand ole' U S of A certainly enhanced my

Death Valley Wild West scene, Stovepipe Wells.

stamina and did wonders to maintain the strength in my arms and shoulders.

After a most enjoyable evening Nigel and I retired to crash out ready for the last day's push. From the start, the push had been extremely hard. It was one hell of a hill to climb! I had to push my chair, from the bed of Death Valley at 280ft below sea level up to the elevation of 5,000feet (one mile high) at Townes Pass, our final destination. The stamina-sapping push took nearly six hours. During a 'pit stop' to repair my blistered, torn and bleeding hands I consumed a pint of water without stopping for breath. My dear friend Tom was reduced to tears on seeing the state of my hands. During the whole of the ascent, Nigel repeatedly poured water over my head and shoulders as the burning heat was almost unbearable. Finally, we reached our goal. As we sat on a little grassy knoll at the top of the hill (which was Townes Pass) we were approached by a lone six foot eight inch-tall motor cyclist. He stopped to chat and as well as Nigel photographing him with our triumphant little quartet, he took a picture of our group as we gathered alongside the signpost bearing the name 'Townes Pass'. My long, exhaustive, but highly successful push across the infamous Death Valley had now been completed.

Before we left the beautiful City of Las Vegas, Nigel and I were taken to meet the City's Mayor Mr Oscar Goodman who presented

Mayor Oscar Goodman presents Swasie with The Key to the City of Las Vegas.

me with 'The Key to the City of Las Vegas'. This indeed was an extremely rare and very prestigious honour to receive. I remain eternally grateful for such a privileged accolade. Our final treat was then being taken to Nevada's Nellis Air Force Base where we witnessed a flying display by America's crack USAF Thunderbirds fighter jets display team (the US equivalent to our RAF Red Arrows). At the conclusion of the display we met the pilots who flew them. Our American stay was certainly one to remember and the result of our fundraising efforts raised over $13,000 for Tom's cancer fund. Not only was I extremely satisfied with such a wonderful result but I also know that my Marje would have been deeply proud of our endeavour.

Nigel and I enjoyed our long return flight to Manchester where we were greeted by a waiting Matron. After a brief chat over a welcome cup of tea I bade farewell to my Bodmin pal and made my way home for a long refreshing sleep.

CHAPTER EIGHTEEN

The Hospitable 'Wheelchair Friendly' Vikings (and the namesake of the 'sprout')

After my latest US visit, my return to England brought me down to earth with a bit of a bump disability wise. I started to take for granted the American policy of 'Disability Awareness' whilst over the 'pond', but here in the UK I quickly realised that we weren't quite in the same league. Remembering my (small) contribution to the British Waterways' suggestion box during my Leeds to Liverpool push, I hoped to shortly repeat this up in the 'land of Tartan'! I had received an invitation to attend the Festival of Fire and Water in June up in Greenock, Scotland. This is a major event involving police, fire and coastguard services which displays the joint skills and capabilities of the emergency services.

Matron and I attended the day's extremely impressive activities which included simulated fire rescues, vehicle displays and helicopter and lifeboat rescues in the harbour. I had previously arranged to follow on the activities by pushing along the Scottish canals from Bishop Briggs to Edinburgh. The charity push was to raise more funds for the Fire Services National Benevolent Fund. I completed the extremely hard push in five long and hard days and met many people along the way who gave generously to my bucket. The push entailed negotiating grassy banks and thick foliage which I had to force my way through, repeating the Leeds to Liverpool scenario. I changed canals at the famous Falkirk Wheel, then pushed on to my final destination, Edinburgh. I informed the authorities of various ways things could be improved and hopefully my recommendations were taken on board. By and large I consider that the appropriate Scottish 'powers that be' are doing all they can to

Swasie at the Falkirk Wheel.

ensure wheelchair friendliness is a priority with regard to recreational, canal access.

At the conclusion of the push I concentrated on my talks, columns and books. These activities consumed my days, assisted by my wheelchair mileage. During this time I was afforded the privilege to sample the warm, courteous and friendly hospitality of the people of Denmark. I received a request to write an article concerning disability awareness and facilities for the physically handicapped in Denmark. This was a fantastic offer! The country is full of places of interest and beauty and is also steeped in tradition and history. With miles of attractive coastline and vast stretches of unspoilt countryside dotted with pretty holiday cottages, historic market towns and fishing harbours, Denmark is also unique for something equally important! The western seaboard area of West Jutland is becoming firmly established as a centre of excellence for visitors with disabilities. Denmark's 'Access for All' initiative was promoted during the 2003 World Travel Market (WTM) event at the Excel Centre in London, to mark the European Year of People with Disabilities (EYPD 2003). This has made West Jutland, around the ferry terminal of Esbjerg, particularly accessible for disabled tourists, with more than 430 different attractions to choose from, including maritime museums and conservation centres. There is even access onto the sandy beaches at some points where ramps and special walkways have been created to make it easier for wheelchair users to get through and beyond the sand dunes and down onto the North sea shore. I would travel to Denmark, accompanied by my *Police News* editor Mrs Chisnall who had received a similar invitation. My article would be written for the *Wirral Champion* and the *Firemark* magazine. After arriving at Harwich, Mrs Chisnall and I boarded the DFDS Tor Line ferry, and enjoyed a pleasant overnight voyage to the Danish port of Esbjerg. The ship, 'Dana Sirena' holds 600 passengers with 200 cabins, some of which are specially adapted for disabled travellers. These are extremely comfortable and afford plenty of room for wheelchairs. Each cabin has a 'wide door' entry, grab rails, adjustable height bed and an emergency alarm call system. Similar disabled toilet facilities are at each country's boarding and disembarking ports. I found boarding the vessel and wheeling my way to my cabin trouble free and assistance was at hand at all times should I have needed it. I found the staff at Harwich terminal's reception to be warm, friendly and courteous as well as highly professional. Likewise, the crew of the Dana Sirena could not do enough to ensure their passengers' welfare and comfort throughout the trip. Lifts on the vessel are spacious and efficient and easily found. They are also easy to enter and leave in a wheelchair. The ship's two al a carte or buffet restaurants are of excellent quality and diners want for nothing. The varied cuisine is a gastronomic delight after which one can relax and enjoy a drink in the comfortable lounge bar. My en-suite cabin proved to be perfect, with safe ablution facilities for disabled people. At the end of our most pleasant trip we disembarked and were met by our Danish host Malte and his British opposite number Andrew. We were joined by the rest of our small party of British writers totalling five in all, each of whom would be writing a feature on our 'assessing disability awareness' trip for our individual papers or magazines. Our little group consisted of three wheelchair users, a heroic ex-helicopter pilot Andy, Mrs Margaret Hydes and myself. We also had our very own Danish translator, the lovely Ann Divinge, a fellow amputee who possesses a tremendous sense of humour.

Although the weather was wet and breezy on our arrival, we all looked forward to our week long 'journalistic' and exploratory tour of beautiful Denmark, and what its revelations regarding standards of disability facilities would be. Our first night's stay was at the wheelchair friendly Hotel Fjordgarden. The following day the weather improved and we all made the short trip by local ferry from Esbjerg to the island of Fano where I stayed in a holiday cottage specially adapted for people with disabilities. Visiting the island of Fano is a must. It is so pretty, with its thatched cottages and quiet lanes as well as a beautiful beach with areas specifically for bird watching. For those who prefer self catering on Fano there is a picturesque seventeenth century Sonderho Kro Inn which offers the kind of hospitality that makes a holiday really special. I also visited a 'home from home'; a very well equipped chalet style house at Ribe Byferie. This is a large self catering holiday centre close to the town centre of historic Ribe which is a 30 minute drive from Esbjerg. I also visited and enjoyed the sights of Ribe's beautiful Cathedral and the nearby Viking Centre, where I enjoyed authentic 'Viking' lunches of venison and berries with smoked cheese, fish and vegetables which are served on request. The food is eaten using Viking implements to consume vast amounts of mead. I thought the

town's museum was particularly well laid out with thousands of
ancient finds classified neatly, so that it was possible to absorb a little
extra information about the area without feeling like hard study.
Ribe Cathedral, built in 1175 is now accessible to people in
wheelchairs. Inside the oldest tombs and timbers complete with
more recent stained glass features by Carl Henning Pedersen.
Pushing around the centre of Ribe I discovered the 'Hotel Dagmar',
Denmark's oldest hotel, built in 1581. Here, I joined the night
watchman on his 'safety tour of inspection' around the city to check
on the flood levels. The quaint cobbled streets were sometimes
difficult, but I managed to negotiate them okay in my wheelchair.
It was here that I met and made a new friend, Police Superintendent
Bjarne Askolm Neilsen who greeted me looking resplendent in his
smart uniform. The Super kindly presented me with a Police
Superintendent's cap, a gift from my new Danish 'colleague' which
I shall truly treasure. We were joined by a representative of the Ribe
Tourist Board, an attractive lady by the name of Tanja Schwartz.
All the beautiful and interesting venues I saw are well worth visiting
and again, I emphasise that those who have any physical disabilities
will have no difficulty exploring and staying at these places. In the
southern part of the region I visited, the authorities can deal with
any special requests or requirements. There is usually no charge for
such services and the equipment available is very extensive.

I visited numerous, well equipped youth hostels in Denmark
which are suitable for disabled visitors and they are mostly larger
than those in the UK, with superb sporting facilities. Whether one
prefers an idyllic individual holiday cottage in a quiet location or
a larger, purpose built self-catering holiday centre with more
amenities, each is available with adaptation to ensure that physically
handicapped visitors are well catered for. I called at many places with
a heritage and long history to more than quench the thirst of those
who wish to avail themselves of the country's colourful past. For
instance, the ancient town of Ribe I have previously referred to goes
right back to Viking times. There is also West Jutland, which is near

Swasie's party enjoy the delights of Danish cuisine.

the picturesque Wadden marshlands. This tidal area (the highest tidal range in the world) teems with all sorts of wildlife and is home to a variety of birds, sea birds and seals. It is also an absolute Mecca for sea anglers. I had a great time at the Wadden Sea Centre which is a great place for children, as it has a multimedia show to highlight the perils of 'when the sea is higher than the land' via a dramatic movie with appropriate sound effects. The town of Ringkobing is also well worth a visit and is where I found fascinating little shops selling various types of souvenirs and amber artefacts.

For information on those who are disabled and their carers, there is a Danish firm called 'Sol Og Strand' who specialise in holiday cottages for disabled visitors to West Jutland. The company divides its holiday homes for wheelchair users into two types. Type one meets the criteria of the 'Dansk Handicap Forbunds' (Danish Union for Disabled Persons). These holiday homes conform to a strict list of requirements with regard to access, entrance and circulation around house, toilet, bathroom and bedroom facilities. Type two are holiday houses selected solely by Sol Og Strand, and are suitable for wheelchair users with a companion or carer. I have visited and seen both and I can recommend each.

My numerous informative visits also included a further place of interest, especially for those in wheelchairs: the Kystcentret at Thyboron. This is the West coast's largest 'discovery' centre. There, you can make you own thunderstorm, start a tornado, make tidal waves or perhaps you may prefer to travel back in geographical time. The centre is open all year round and houses interactive displays to give visitors a 'hands-on' sensory experience of the coastal ecology. Denmark has an ongoing battle to control its eroding coastline and protect its population from the constant threat (in places) of flooding. All this is brought to life with frightening reality via vivid illustration and accompanied by modern, state of the art, sound effects. The centre overlooks the North Sea and gave us visitors a sensory experience of the sea getting as close to us as is possible without actually getting ourselves wet! All of this is available to wheelchair users. I strongly recommend anyone to take such a 'Utopian' holiday, especially those who are physically handicapped, as Denmark will certainly take care of you. I advise those who wish to travel across to this Scandinavian paradise to avail themselves of these venues and facilities. I personally recommend a visit to one of the museums, aquariums, towns and conservation areas I visited where I guarantee your curiosity will be duly rewarded. The Danish people are without doubt extremely courteous, caring, kind and considerate hosts. All those wonderful people I had the privilege of meeting during my stay were truly Ambassadors to their beautiful country, the 'Home of the Viking'! Being a 'wheelchair pilot'

Swasie on patrol with the Danish Night Watchman.

I emphasise to those of a similar 'ilk' that travelling to, and touring, Denmark will present few, if any, problems. The Danish authorities go to great lengths to ensure a visit to their country can be enjoyed by all, especially the disabled fraternity.

Eventually our journalistic mission came to an end, but what an exciting and grossly educational trip it was. My visit to Denmark was a most enlightening and informative experience. I certainly absorbed many ideas and much information as to what could be done to ease and simplify life for the integration of disabled people in a modern society. My Denmark trip was a perfect preparation for my next long distance push.

Within less than two weeks I was off again, this time to Belgium. As the year 2003 was the 'Year of the Disabled' I had worked hard with Lomax and the appropriate authorities of the UK and Belgium to bring about a wheelchair push from the British Houses of Parliament to the Brussels Parliament. As usual, I would be staying with the emergency services. The push was to raise funds for various disability charities. On Thursday 25th September I had the honour of being seen off from Westminster by Miss Maria Eagle, Minister for the Disabled and some of her parliamentary colleagues. With her was Mr Wilmot from Lomax, the press, Mr Dave Webster and a photographer from 'Lipton Ice Tea', another kind sponsor who furnished enough drinks for the whole of my twelve-day push. My Lomax backup driver was this time Brian Chaplin. The push through London and around Hyde Park corner was very intimidating as the heavy traffic was not very sympathetic to the audacious wheelchair who dared to be intruding on their carriageways! The climb out of London was hard, especially up the steep and lengthy Shooters Hill. My day's 26-mile push terminated at Bexley Heath Fire Station where Brian and I enjoyed a hearty dinner and later, a good night's sleep upstairs in the crews' dormitory. The next day's push took me first to Dartford Fire Station where we stopped for refreshment. The Dartford crew met us two miles from their station and escorted us in. My bucket was very heavy due to the

Maria Eagle MP sees Swasie off from Westminster on his long push to Brussells.

continual donations from the generous public. Later, when suitably refreshed, we moved on to complete the day's fundraising push at Stroude. Again we received typical warm and friendly fire service hospitality. During the night Brian caused absolute mayhem amongst the 'troops' with his extremely loud snoring, for which he received a lot of 'stick' during the following morning's breakfast. The next day would take us to Chatham, Sittingbourne and finally Faversham, a partly retained fire station where we were to sleep on the station floor. The following morning Brian and I were escorted for three miles by a retained crew who came in specially to escort us. Later, during the day's push we stopped at Canterbury Fire Station for a hot meal before making our way to Dover Fire Station where we would spend our last night before boarding the ferry.

After a pleasant trip over to Dunkirk we made off through France to our next starting venue, Ostend. After a long drive we eventually arrived at the town where we were met and escorted by a police car to our overnight accommodation at Ostend Fire Station. Although it was late evening when we arrived, that did not diminish the extremely warm and enthusiastic welcome by our hosts. These comprised of local officials, senior police and fire officers and members of the IPA (International Police Association). After formal introductions were completed, Brian and I were seated at a table and furnished with some much-needed food. An inevitable press and photo shoot ensued before we could finally make for our beds.

After breakfast the following morning, Brian and I were given a tour of Ostend by senior fire officers. Finally, after more photos and interviews, Brian and I set off accompanied by a fire truck and an armed *politie* officer. The push went well and amazingly, I received donations from fascinated members of the public as well as motorists. Eventually I arrived at Gwent and the overwhelming welcome was totally unexpected. I was greeted on arrival by TV, radio and press. A lone piper also joined me to walk to the town centre, playing a welcoming lament as we made our way along.

This soon generated a large, interested crowd. The TV cameraman filmed me pushing until I reached my goal at the town's large police station. There I was presented with a police shield, a fire medal and a commemorative plaque. Brian too received a plaque for his efforts. The ensuing period was consumed by interviews at the conclusion of which we were taken to our hotel. Later, after a most welcome dinner, I savoured the sheer luxury of a hot bath before making for my bed.

After a continental breakfast (which wouldn't fill a sparrow) I joined my escort of two *politie* cyclists and a fire truck and commenced my long push to distant Brussels. The weather had been kind so far and I continued making progress. After fifteen miles, I stopped at a police station in the little town of Aalst to chat to my Belgian 'colleagues' before continuing onto Aalst Fire Station. After celebratory drinks, interviews and the proverbial cuppa I left my kind hosts and resumed my push. I continued to receive abundant donations from everyone I passed as by now the whole country was aware of my wheelchair endeavour. As I reached the outskirts of Brussels I was met by the local IPA President and we made for the massive Brussels Fire Station complex. An extremely large and tumultuous welcome greeted Brian and I as we rolled along the last hundred yards to the station. After a hearty meal and much chat we then moved on to our overnight accommodation at the equally large police training complex two miles away. Here we were given the privilege of the Officers' suite.

The next morning Brian and I were taken to the studios of Radio Brussels where I was interviewed live on air. This gave me the golden opportunity to thank profusely the wonderful people of Belgium for their extremely warm hospitality. Brian and I were then whisked across town to be interviewed by even more TV, press and radio crews.

The whole endeavour was a resounding fundraising success as well as being a totally successful PR exercise for all the services involved. The event was concluded after Brian and I met members of the Belgian equivalent to our SAS during a simulated siege exercise. We were also given a fearsome display as to the awesome power of their water cannon. Our stay was concluded by our long drive back to Dunkirk and then on over the channel back to 'Blighty', courtesy of the ship, the Dawn Merchant. This brought the year's foreign endeavours to an end.

The new year brought about two exciting encounters, one of which was when Matron and I were invited to take part in the popular television show Ready Steady Cook. I was 'Red Tomato' and Matron was 'Green Pepper'. My chef was Phil Vickery, husband of the TV star Fern Britton and Matron's chef was James Martin.

Swasie and Matron with Phil Vicory, James Martin and Ainsley Harriott on TV's *Ready, Steady Cook*.

We were hosted by the show's presenter Ainsley Harriott. Our hosts were terrific and the show was fantastic. We both enjoyed a truly wonderful day at the Shepherds Bush television studios down in London. The other important encounter happened on Sunday 29th February when Mrs Chisnall and I attended a wheelchair event and met my friend Dame Tanni Grey-Thompson, the wheelchair Olympic Gold medallist. Despite being so busy with all my engagements, I was already making preparations for my next major endeavour abroad.

CHAPTER NINETEEN

Reaching for the Sky

This time my destination was the remote island of Saint Helena hidden in the wastes of the South Atlantic Ocean. My intended task was to ascend the infamous 'Jacob's Ladder' on the island, with my wheelchair! Matron and I travelled from Brize Norton to Ascension Island and from there we travelled across the distant horizon by ship (the RMS St. Helena) to the isolation of the beautiful tropical island of the same name. The voyage is a mini cruise through warm, clear waters. Dolphins swim and play alongside the ship and flying fish look like little sparrows flitting alongside the vessel as we plough through the turquoise ocean. Occasionally, the unmistakable fin of a shark can be seen cutting the surface. Matron and I had a beautiful cabin stewardess named Lina who looked after our needs and welfare throughout our Southbound voyage; Lina was voted 'Miss Saint Helena' shortly after the conclusion of the trip to the island.

The whole trip to and from Ascension down to Saint Helena is truly an exciting, wonderful and extremely enjoyable journey. The island of Saint Helena is a volcanic outcrop 10,000 miles from the UK and the island's inhabitants are the most friendly and hospitable of people. It is an island of contrast with a wind-eroded desert to vivid emerald hillsides, including pastures and lush vegetation-filled valleys. The coastline is bronze coloured, as a result of volcanic residue, with cliffs towering as high as 1,000 feet, their base carved by centuries of pounding Atlantic rollers. There is no airport and the island can only be reached by ship. This little paradise became a British dependency in 1834 and still retains its nineteenth century values. The island is steeped in 300 years of colonial history which is manifested in the architecture and ambience of Jamestown, the capital. The town is a Georgian seaport and is well protected by eighteenth century fortifications and is abundantly endowed with a living heritage from its early days. Jamestown sits in a deep, narrow valley and houses the seat of Government and a magnificent museum, as well as hotels and shops. The route out of Jamestown is by two steep routes: Side Path and Ladder Hill. For the more adventurous (such as 'yours truly'!) there is the infamous Jacob's Ladder. This is a steep (beyond 45%) 900ft climb of 700 steps cut into the cliff face from sea level to the top of Ladder Hill.

The island was discovered in May 1505 by the Portuguese admiral Joa da Nova on his return voyage from India. He named the island in memory of Saint Helena, the mother of Emperor Constantine. Due to the vegetation and copious amounts of fruit on the island it soon became a haven for sea travellers, but not for wheelchairs! The island's hills are fiercely steep and long and I found them to be most wheelchair unfriendly. Sufferers of scurvy would be deposited onto the island to benefit from the citrus fruits that abound, before being collected later by another ship on their subsequent recovery. The islanders are known as 'Saints' and possess a unique and special charm. They are all descendants of British settlers sent out by the East India Company, slaves and indentured workers from Africa and the East. No doubt it is this unique combination that has generated and brought about the Saints' amazing captivating, and extremely kind and friendly nature. Many famous names have visited Saint Helena over the centuries including Darwin, Halley, Captain Bligh and Captain Cook. Napoleon Bonaparte was exiled to the island in 1815 following his defeat at the battle of Waterloo. He lived among the beautiful foliage, exotic tropical flowers, coffee plants and banana trees at Longwood House until his death in 1821. Matron and I couldn't resist regularly sampling and consuming large amounts of such delightful citrus fruits and coffee during our stay on the beautiful island. The residence is now a museum owned by the French Government.

The island began issuing stamps in 1856 and the 'Discovery' issue was released in the year of my Marje's premature death, in 1997. The island is nearly eleven miles long and six and a half miles wide. It is blessed with enviable, constantly warm tropical temperatures. The early fortifications, set in the most beautiful and spectacular scenery, give evidence as to its fascinating heritage. Although I found negotiating the many footpaths of 'discovery' to be difficult (and sometimes dangerous!), the breathtaking rewards were phenomenal on seeing the superb examples of the island's endemic flora and fauna. I also satisfied my insatiable lust for sea fishing as copious amounts of tuna, marlin and barracuda are in abundance in the deep waters around the island. The food here is superb, as Saint Helena has developed its own unique, multi-ethnic cuisine which Matron and I enjoyed immensely. There are a number of eating places on the island including the Consulate Hotel, Wellington House and Ann's Place; Matron's and my preferred watering hole! The food is a gastronomical delight for all, especially those regular visitors, the 'round the world' yachters! On arrival at the beautiful island paradise, Matron and I completed customs formalities before we were met by the island's Deputy Police Chief, Merlin George and his policewoman sergeant, Julie Balchin. The two then kindly showed us to our accommodation in Jamestown to drop our luggage off, before we returned to the Jamestown Police Station to meet our various hosts. My ascent of the infamous 'ladder' would take place in a few days and my intention was to raise much needed funds for the Jamestown Hospital. Every person I spoke to was adamant that there was no way I would get to the top of the 900ft structure with my wheelchair. I was quietly confident, but the more the islanders insisted such an ascent could *not* be done, I started to wonder if they knew something specific that would prevent me from completion. Many suggested I go to inspect the Ladder prior to my attempt, but I never do this with any of my endeavours. I always take whatever the challenge is, head on. The reason for this is to prevent me getting second thoughts if my prior inspection was to put me off. I would ascend the structure on the day and in the meantime, I would stay away from it.

Although the harbour, shops and police station were only half a mile from our flat and it was an easy 'roll' down through the town, the return trip was extremely hard. The town is built on a long gradient and all roads and paths out of Jamestown mean negotiating very steep inclines. The town is approximately a mile and a half long and each day I rolled down to the harbour, then pushed the return journey to the hospital at the top end of the town. I did this a couple of times per day to maintain my strength and stamina, as I knew I would need both when I made my ascent of the Ladder!

During the couple of days prior to the climb, Matron and I were taken on many tours around and across the island where we met many new friends. We visited a coffee and banana plantation owned by Mr and Mrs Reg Yon, who presented us with a large bunch of green bananas and a quantity of ground coffee; Matron is an ardent coffee addict, and connoisseur! I was pleasantly surprised when the bananas turned bright yellow within two days. They tasted unique and their special flavour differed from any other bananas I have tasted.

Notices announcing my fundraising ascent of the Ladder were posted throughout the whole of the island, even on trees and road signs. I expected to raise about £250 (if I was successful) and this would go in its entirety to the Jamestown Hospital. Every day when I wandered through the capital I was greeted warmly by a gentleman wearing what I thought was a priest's 'dog collar' as I passed the Catholic church. He would greet me each time with, 'Good morning my son' and gesticulate with his hand in the sign of the cross. I would reply respectfully, 'Good morning Father'. One day the Father told me that 'You are a good man, the Lord will be proud of what you are doing for us my son'. I informed him that I was not a good man and I was not a Catholic. I elaborated by saying that I tried to be a good man but, like everyone else, I had had my 'moments' during my lifetime! 'Why, what have you done that's not

The infamous Jacob's Ladder, Saint Helena Island.

good?' he persisted. I informed him that I was not going to give him any 'incriminating confessions' and resumed my journey. After a couple of days I saw him come out of the church with a lady. I was with Matron and we both bid them good morning. I said, 'Good morning Father, is the lady your secretary?' The priest took me to one side and informed me, 'Swasie, I'll have to tell you, I'm not a priest – I'm the town's bloody dentist'! We both fell about laughing as I realised his 'dog collar' was in fact a light blue sweat shirt with a white ringed collar. We all had a great laugh at the innocent deception!

The day of the ascent arrived, Saturday 1st May. As I meandered down to the starting point I saw the lady who owned Ann's Place where Matron and I enjoyed eating excellent island cuisine. Every time I saw her about the town she would shout, 'You *won't* do it you know'! This day she came to me and bet me five pounds I wouldn't get to the top. Undeterred, I arrived at the foot of the structure ready for my historic climb of Saint Helena's awesome Jacob's Ladder. I was filmed, photographed and interviewed by a reporter from the *Saint Helena Herald*. All my police and fire friends were present; Police Chief Derek Thomas, his deputy Merlin and members of the Saint Helena Government were all there to witness the spectacle. They all thought it would not be completed – I was determined to prove them all wrong. It seemed as if the whole of the island's population turned out to witness the climb. I was touched by the numerous children and even some adults who crowded around me seeking my autograph, or wanted to be pictured alongside me. I was truly humbled yet exceedingly proud. Marje was uppermost in my mind and I knew I must not fail!

I grabbed the rails on each side of the structure. The steps were at least a foot high, and as a 'frontal attack' was not the best way to make my ascent with the chair, I decided to go up backwards! Police Sergeant Darlene Peters and Deputy Chief Merlin George accompanied me, and the Chief himself saw me off from the base. The majority of my climb was on my bottom pulling my 47lb chair up with me. I would drag myself up by the rail with one hand, pulling my chair with the other. I sweated extensively in the searing heat of the tropical sun. I was kindly fed plentiful amounts of water as well as having it thrown over me. As I climbed higher and higher, I knew there was no going back. I could now see from my elevated position, the massive crowds that had gathered, filling Jamestown almost to capacity. As I struggled on, I knew Marje was with me and this made me determined to make it. Matron was also a matter of feet below, photographing almost every step I completed.

Suddenly I heard loud cheering and I stopped to look up. I couldn't believe it; I was only twenty feet from the top and there were crowds awaiting my arrival at the 'summit'. This gave me a tremendous adrenaline boost and although I felt shattered, I didn't feel the last gruelling few feet. I arrived at the little aperture in the wall at the top and pushed my chair ahead of me, then rolled onto my back with a feeling of elation and relief. The noise of the welcoming crowd was deafening. I was unceremoniously dragged up and thrown into my chair and smothered in hugs, handshakes and pats on the back. It was phenomenal! Men, women and children were all vying to shake my hand. Some were pouring litres of water from bottles and cans all over me, and some furnished bottles of iced water for me to drink. The latter never touched the sides as it went down!

I could see the roof of a police Landrover behind the crowd and then Chief Derek Thomas threaded his way through to offer me his congratulations. I felt as though I was dreaming. Someone crouched down and spoke into my ear, his soft Irish brogue said, 'Well done my son!' – it was none other than the 'town's 'dentist' Mr Michael Gilmore! He took my hand and shook it vigorously, 'Well done Swasie, there's a lot here who didn't think you'd do it' he said. I sat there for twenty enjoyable minutes, savouring each second. Finally Chief Thomas told me he would drive me down to Jamestown with my wheelchair in the back of the Landrover. I wouldn't hear of it. When I said I was going back down with my chair via the ladder the crowd became almost silent with disbelief. I was informed that going

The view from the top of Jacob's Ladder.

up was bad enough, but going down was more dangerous. I manoeuvred to the top step, holding the rails tightly. I looked down almost a thousand feet. I couldn't believe that I had actually ascended what I was looking down at. There, far below at what looked like an almost vertical angle, was distant Jamestown. I knew that I would have to keep an almost superhuman grip on those handrails, as one slip and it would be an unrecoverable free fall of 900ft. Once everyone knew I was determined to return to the town via the route I had ascended, a number of volunteers insisted that they went down ahead 'just in case'! One of those who went back down in front of me was Matron.

It was possibly harder going down as I could not afford to slacken my iron grip of those side rails. As a consequence, I burned both hands as they took virtually all my fourteen stone weight plus the 47-pound weight of the chair. After what seemed an eternity I neared the masses at the base. I stopped and somehow lifted my chair high above my head in victory and the crowd went wild with enthusiastic encouragement. I shouted at the top of my voice, 'Ann from Ann's Place had bet me five *hundred* pounds I wouldn't do it'! From somewhere amongst the mass of humanity I heard Ann's hysterical reply, 'I did *not* you liar, I said five pounds!' Everyone fell about laughing at Ann's red-faced denial. We all took it in good fun. On reaching the ground the same euphoric welcome was repeated by all those present. I was absolutely mobbed. I was hugged, kissed, slapped and my hand was repeatedly grabbed and shaken with congratulations. I loved *every* minute of the crowd's affection. Matron was presented with a bunch of exotic coloured 'Bird of Paradise' flowers. Police Chief Thomas presented me (a non-drinker) with a magnum of champagne.

The collecting tins which had been deposited throughout the island before the event were duly returned to the police station, and each was full. I gave an illustrated talk the same evening at the Police Club at the top of Ladder Hill. The resulting count of donations received was over £2,500; this was a phenomenal amount as money

Swasie receives a tumultuous welcome on his return to base.

is at an absolute premium for the majority of the island's inhabitants. A further £250 was forthcoming from Captain Rodney Young and his crew of the RMS St Helena. In the days that followed Matron and I were invited to lunch by the Saint Helena Government. We were both subsequently invited to dinner at Plantation House, the Governor's residence, by His Excellency the Governor John Styles and his charming wife Lynette.

The ascent and descent of Saint Helena Island's infamous Jacob's Ladder was a financially resounding success for the Jamestown Hospital. The day after the ladder event, I was approached by a tearful lady who had suffered a mastectomy after being diagnosed with having breast cancer. The lady (I shall call her Jane) apologised for possibly causing me distress, as she knew my wife had died from cancer, but she virtually pleaded with me for help. She unbuttoned her blouse and showed me her bra, one cup of which was filled with crumpled newspaper to represent the missing breast. She explained that there were others on the island like her and none could afford a proper cosmetic breast prosthesis. She said she had lost her womanhood and described herself as feeling 'de-womanised'. She explained that even if she and those like her could afford the £100 the prostheses cost, there were none on the island; they would have to be sought from the UK or South Africa and this would increase the cost further. I was asked if I could assist those desperate ladies to eliminate their frustrated indignity. I listened sympathetically and I too was almost reduced to tears as my own vivid memory of Marje's similar predicament was, and is, still very sore.

I promised 'Jane' (who is now a lifelong friend of Matron and me) that I would do my vehement utmost to obtain and ship the items so urgently needed down to the island as soon as I could get them. I promised her (and myself) that I would give this very touching request my undivided attention; on my return to the UK this would be my utmost priority. I had a few 'irons in the fire' and a few sources I could approach for help in this matter.

Matron and I subsequently returned to Ascension where we spent a happy few days before finally returning home to Wirral to resume our life of normality. My next move would be to get in touch with Clatterbridge Hospital Breast Clinic and seek their urgent help for my friends on distant Saint Helena Island. My imminent illustrated talks would, for the moment, be to raise extra cash for the Jamestown Hospital. The first item on my fundraising agenda was to start a new account with my bank called the Saint Helena Jacob's Ladder Fund. I would build this up to assist my endeavours to beg, borrow or even purchase medical items for the island's hospital and its patients. My determination in this field matched that of my climb of Jacob's Ladder!

CHAPTER TWENTY

Restoration of Confidence and Happiness

Even though I had resumed my pushes and talks on my return from Saint Helena, I contacted various places as promised to see if I could help the island further. As explained, my first port of call was to Clatterbridge Breast Clinic. The brilliant and extremely sympathetic staff listened intently to my sad renditions regarding the ladies of Saint Helena. Without any hesitation, every member of the breast clinic team offered their unreserved help and assistance to further my cause. Within no time I was furnished with breast prostheses of all sizes and proportions that would cater from young girls, to obese old ladies. I obtained a large box from Lomax which would normally house a wheelchair, and this was filled with the precious breast prostheses as well as nebulisers, blood monitoring machines and other equally valuable medical items that were so ardently sought in Jamestown. I then contacted Mr Derek Kaye at Andrew Weir Shipping who immediately offered to have the consignment of important items collected from my home and shipped to Saint Helena free of charge.

This was the start of something I now regularly perform. As soon as I obtain or accumulate any medical items, they are then shipped down to the 'Saints'. I followed the breast prostheses with a large consignment of orthopaedic prostheses, dressings, heart monitors and other ancillary medical items across a wide spectrum. Whenever I have gathered sufficient items for shipment, Andrew Weir unhesitatingly collects and ships them to the island free of charge. Similarly, I managed to swell the Saint Helena account to over £3,500, which is there should I need to purchase any items for the

Swasie's medical items being collected from his home for shipment to Saint Helena Hospital.

hospital. The island's Health Minister, Mrs Ivy Ellick, contacted me to say that the hospital urgently needed adjustable orthopaedic beds. These are an expensive item indeed. I contacted the suppliers in the UK but they would not give me any concessions. I then contacted the manufacturers who offered me one such bed (which cost £1,800) for £500. I audaciously asked if I could buy 'three for £900', never dreaming that they would agree. However, not only did they kindly agree, they had them collected by Andrew Weir and shipped down to the island. I dipped into the fund and sent the appropriate cheque to the manufacturer. I personally would like to express my deep gratitude to Andrew Weir for their truly benevolent and ongoing assistance. Among all my friends, associates and contacts, I hold those on the Island of Saint Helena very dear. I just can't do enough for them. I intend to financially support (via the fund) the island's disabled association to hopefully better their standards of care. Another extremely prestigious venue I am now regularly invited to attend is Birkenhead School. This school is the Oxford of Birkenhead. Here are furnished the country's future academics, doctors, surgeons, and lawyers, and to be invited to give a regular address here is without doubt a great privilege. The extremely generous students and staff ensure that my bucket if filled to the brim when I visit.

I am regularly blessed with receiving letters and emails from the ladies of Saint Helena, especially 'Jane'. I am extremely proud of such correspondence as in a way; I believe that I am assisting via 'my Marje' who went through what they are experiencing. 'Jane' in particular regularly (and embarrassingly) expresses her gratitude for my efforts which, she says 'have restored her femininity'. What a fantastic compliment. I am humbled but proud of the result of my endeavours, and because of the amount of money raised it pleases me that I have helped 'Jane' to overcome her ongoing, depressive frustration. I continually maintain my monitoring of the hospital and its patients on that far away island.

My heavy involvement with Hunter Company continues and I attend the Royal Marines Commando Training Centre every sixteen weeks or so. My dedicated and total commitment to the young men of Hunter Company knows absolutely no bounds. I have completed many awesome endurance courses and gruelling marches of 30 miles, uphill speed marches as well as the notorious 'Exe Descent': a 32-mile canoe paddle from Tiverton to Exeter down the fast and turbulent waters of the River Exe. During this, we were all thrown out into the 'oggin' and I too was swept away under the 'Bridge over Troubled Waters' at Bickleigh. These physically demanding endeavours are always followed by an illustrated address to those who are at the time unable to take part in the physical side

Swasie on Marines' river Exe Descent.

due to their early stages of recovery. One of my most prized possessions is my coveted Royal Marines green 'lid' which I wear with immense pride on every occasion I can. I am involved with RMR (Royal Marines Reserve), Merseyside as well as the Royal Marine cadets. I have a lot of time for the country's youngsters who take the trouble to join the various cadet corps. Each year, without fail I join the ranks for the eleventh hour of the eleventh month's Remembrance Day parade, representing my beloved Hunter Company RM.

My ongoing efforts were further acknowledged and enhanced early in 2005 when I was contacted by Mr Nik Demetriades who

Swasie representing Hunter Company RM Lympstone at Remembrance Parade with Royal Marine Cadets.

invited to become Patron of an extremely worthy children's charity, the 'Enable Me' project down in sunny Sussex. This is a new partnership on the South coast that is bringing schoolchildren and local government together to raise awareness of disability issues. The Enable Me project is being run by 3 Towns Shopmobility, the charity which provides wheelchairs and scooters in town centres to make shopping easier for people with mobility problems. My tasks involve me visiting schools and talking to children of all ages in my quest to educate them as to Disability Awareness. I enjoy this involvement immensely and many of the children I meet are truly inspirational to my ongoing efforts. My daily 'workload' still involves writing my columns, writing my books, giving 'after dinner' talks and undertaking lengthy wheelchair pushes, either for charity or maintaining my training schedule. This scenario is all worked around my attendances at Lympstone, Royal Marines Training Centre and, as from my acceptance of being the children's Patron, Littlehampton, Bognor and Worthing. The saying that 'there aren't enough hours in the day' really *is* true! However, I would not have it any other way! My involvement with the Enable Me project brings home to me just how important this is. As well as linking in with the schools the venture also involves statutory and voluntary organisations and residents of Bognor Regis, Littlehampton and Worthing – hence the title '3 *Towns* Shopmobility' – uniting with a joint aim to raise awareness and build long-term relationships with new partners, supporters and fundraisers. Enable Me is about promoting social inclusion and fostering a better understanding of disability issues, so that the Shopmobility scheme is not just seen as a service for the elderly. The message is very much that disability and temporary or long-term mobility problems can actually effect anyone of any age, and as a result wheelchairs and scooter services are available to all. To generate much needed finance for the project, I took part in a three-day charity wheelchair push from Bognor Regis to Littlehampton and on to Worthing. I was accommodated at the fire services establishment at Marine Court; the therapeutic 'haven' for firefighters and their families. Much of the push was along the coastal road or sea front, and I even had to negotiate grassy paths and pebble beaches in places! After a press interview and a photo shoot on the Bognor sea front I set off on my lengthy trek on Wednesday 18th May, with a cameraman walking alongside me to film my progress. For the first half mile I was 'escorted' along the sea front by a number of volunteers on their Shopmobility electric scooters. The weather was superb – bright and sunny with a slight cooling sea breeze. After losing my escorts I continued on for nine miles with my cameraman for company. The local radio had already broadcast details of my coastal push which brought donations from motorists, traffic wardens and shoppers as I meandered along. Eventually, after four and a half hours of non-stop pushing I arrived at Barnham Primary School, which has a special needs unit for children suffering from various disabilities, including learning difficulties.

I was deafened on my arrival when I was afforded a tumultuous welcome by the school's head teacher Mrs Julie Hodgson, her staff, teachers and pupils; many of those gathered were disabled. I spent some time inside the school drawing pictures with, and for, the children. After a refreshing cuppa, I pushed on to Littlehampton, escorted for part of the way by two students. Eventually I completed the day's push of nearly twenty miles and arrived to another warm welcome at Littlehampton Community School. On leaving the school I made my way through the town to meet the Mayor, Mr Malcom Belchamber MBE. After this I returned to my overnight accommodation at Marine Court.

The following day was not so kind weather wise, as I set off into the morning rain bound for Worthing. I was filmed by a BBC news crew as I negotiated the numerous puddles along the windy sea front. I was soaked in no time and as well as the wind and rain, today I had the additional struggle over sand, pebbles and then the notorious Kingston Gorse. In good weather, this would be a wonderful, scenic venue but today, it was vastly different. The particular route was also very wheelchair unfriendly! As the rain came down in sheets I was confronted by a closed gate. I rolled out of my chair and picked it up and dropped it over the fence and crawled under the wire to get back into my seat on its now, soaking wet cushion. My accompanying film cameraman was also having difficulty preventing the rain from damaging his camera. I pushed along through the grass and down the numerous dips along the Gorse, passing the rear of some very expensive houses with a number of high profile celebrities. After more than a mile I was confronted by a six-foot high fence in which there was a door. Again, the door was wheelchair non-negotiable! I had to 'bale out' onto the wet mud and lift my chair up and over the fence. I then crawled through the mud

Swasie is welcomed by children of 'The Orchard' at Barnham Primary School, Sussex.

to rejoin my chair on the other side. This was most uncomfortable, inconvenient and damned hard but it was good film footage for the cameraman. I'm glad he thought so! The rain did not let up and I was thoroughly soaked through to the skin and freezing cold due to the incessant wind. Finally I reached the rest of my team who were waiting for me outside the Sea Lane Café on Goring seafront. I wish to draw attention to the fact that, for people in wheelchairs, here was another major problem. To enter the café I had to drag my chair up steep, cold, wet steps to reach the café entrance. My struggles were also being filmed and photographed by two students and would be shown at the official Enable Me launch the following evening.

Negotiating the steps was extremely difficult and dangerous. Many times this establishment had sought planning permission to erect a ramp to enable access for people such as myself. To date, all planning permission applications for this have been refused! I eventually managed to propel my sodden self into the warm, dry confines of the crowded café where I ravenously consumed a couple of bacon sandwiches and a mug of hot tea. Amazingly, most people in there were aware of who I was and what I was up to. I received many generous donations from the café's patrons and also the kindly staff. As I left to resume my push along the wet and windy coastline, I was again filmed 'negotiating' the steps. This time I fell out of my chair and we both crashed down onto the ground below. Everyone rushed to try and help but I hit the ground before they could get to me. This was entirely my own fault because I had refused numerous offers of help prior to my descent. However, I reiterate my point: I should have had the entitlement of a ramp to facilitate a safe exit from the establishment. I hope the new Discrimination against the Disabled Act legislation will now eliminate the Café's ongoing fight to obtain this important facility. Having lived on the seat of my pants for the past nine years, I feel people who are disabled or physically handicapped in one way or another, especially those of us in wheelchairs, should, and could, fare a lot better.

Nursing a cut and a few bruises I resumed my push towards Worthing and after only a short distance I was intercepted by two kind cyclists who each gave me a ten-pound note for my bucket. The rain and the wind offered no respite as I battled along the seafront towards my destination. I made for the town centre where the town's Mayor, Mr Jack Saheid, and his press entourage awaited my arrival. Officials from the 3 Towns Mobility and Enable Me charities joined the throng together with police and senior fire officers. Finally, after filming, press interviews and photographs were concluded, I retreated to the nearby 3 Towns offices where I washed and changed into dry clothing. After returning to Marine Court and enjoying a hot meal, it wasn't long before I was into my bed and

Swasie receives a wet and windy 'Mayoral' welcome at Worthing.

almost instantly asleep. The following evening saw the official launch of the charity of which I am the privileged Patron. Enable Me was officially launched at Worthing Assembly Hall on Friday 20th May, and was attended by 200 invited guests. As Patron I had the privilege of joining the company of the Lord Lieutenant of West Sussex Mr Hugh Wyatt, His Grace the Duke of Richmond, Her Grace the Duchess of Norfolk and Mr Nick Gibb MP. The packed audience included local head teachers, students, pupils, school governors and educational consultants. Local Mayors, Town, Borough and district councillors, trustees and service users filled every nook and cranny of the conference centre. One of my main sponsors, 'Level Access Lifts' catered for those of us who were in wheelchairs getting onto the large elevated stage to give our individual address. I was more than delighted to assist the firm's proprietor Mr Nick Dade as he made his final adjustments to ensure that safety and comfort was paramount to the wheelchair occupants using the lift. Hannah McGrath, Worthing's first Junior Mayor and also the deputy Head Girl at Davison C of E High school for girls, gave an interesting rendition about how the Enable Me project started at her school the year before (2004) as a citizenship project. It was Helen who actually coined the phrase Enable Me which was her response to experiencing many years of frustration while bringing up her son David, now nineteen, who has a rare form of muscular dystrophy. It was because of her own experiences as a mother that Helen became passionate about how society needs to find ways of enabling the disabled to become positive. The public needed educating about not using negative terms to stigmatise those who suffered various disabilities. This is precisely the scenario I have persistently and pedantically described throughout this book. All too often I experience exactly this frustrating and annoying, inconsiderate attitude.

The formal launch went well and after an enjoyable meal the evening was concluded after interesting and emotional addresses were given by His Grace the Duke of Richmond, Her Grace the Duchess of Norfolk and the Lord Lieutenant followed by other dignitaries. A tutor from the Lavinia Norfolk Centre, (a 'Special unit' of Angmering school) Mr Ben Locke, and one of the teenage pupils, Alex McGrory, both of whom are wheelchair users, gave personal renditions about inclusion and what it *really* means to each of them being disabled and confined to a wheelchair. Neither pulled any punches as they each explained in graphic detail what it is like to have been given the brilliant opportunity to attend and teach at a mainstream school with able-bodied students, because now they don't experience the negative effects of social exclusion from their colleagues and fellow students.

I have found my involvement with schools, youth groups and the younger generation in general to be extremely rewarding as they are truly 'ambassadorial' to their generation. They seem to possess disability awareness almost naturally. One of my life's biggest bonuses is having met and befriended a young man called Jamie who has a large brain tumour. This young man always insists on meeting me whenever I am down at Littlehampton. Not only that, he always requires being pushed alongside me as I undertake a charity push in his area, however ill he may be. I deem it an utter privilege to be included in his circle of friends. Jamie is a true inspiration to me. Four weeks later dawned Saturday 11th June 2005; this was an extremely

The Enable Me charity launch.

memorable and special day! On this day I received the *ultimate* accolade; I was made an MBE in Her Majesty the Queen's birthday honours. I was over the moon! I immediately dedicated this high honour to my wife Marjorie. My elation knew no bounds and this gave me the incentive to ensure that my fundraising efforts would continue on unabated. To commemorate my award I gave a celebratory evening at Wallasey Masonic Hall three weeks later for over 200 invited guests. My new, elevated status brought about further invitations and requests to attend various venues to give 'after dinner' addresses at 'black tie' functions, open charity shops and schools and hospitals. All of these engagements enhanced the contents of my fundraising bucket considerably. More visits to 'my Hunter Company' at Lympstone and Enable Me talks to schools in Sussex followed as well as my daily pushes and visits to Marje.

Eventually the day of my Palace investiture arrived, Friday 28th October. Matron, Jo and I travelled down to the London Metropolis where we stayed at the Union Jack Club prior to our major event the following day. The three of us were up with the lark and after a hearty breakfast made for the Palace. On arrival we were ushered through the large gates and crunched our way across the pink gravel forecourt. Jo, Matron and I were then courteously escorted by a footman inside the Palace. Jo and Matron were to be seated in the Throne Room while I was taken to a separate room with others to be invested. I felt as though the whole scenario was a dream. I was extremely emotional and I thought how very proud Marje would now be. My sentiments were shared by my tearful and totally mesmerised daughter. It was Jo's very first glimpse of the capital, and *what* a reason for such a first visit to London! I was the only wheelchair person to be invested on the day and when my turn came to present myself before His Royal Highness Prince Charles, my chest filled with pride as I wheeled past Jo and Matron sitting feet away on the front row. I was extremely proud when the Prince invested me with my MBE. As I chatted to him I felt a lump in my throat and had tears of pride in my eyes. His Highness informed that

Her Majesty was very impressed by my 210-mile wheelchair push to the Palace with her letters and gifts during the year of her Golden Jubilee. He went on to say that she had found *my* personal gift, the book *Wheelchair Pilot*, to be 'extremely interesting'. I was asked where my strength and inspiration came from to perform such feats. I immediately replied without any hesitation, 'From my beloved late wife Marjorie Sir'!

In October, at the request of Arrowe Park hospital's physiotherapy unit I became involved with an amputee who had 'given up the ghost' after having his leg removed. I was asked if I could attempt to help the patient by being in his company and

His Royal Highness Prince Charles invests Swasie with his MBE.

Jo, Matron and Swasie at the Palace.

hopefully help to restore his confidence and morale. When I met the man, named Bill, he was at an extreme low and was suffering an almost fatal depression. I visited Bill every day for a month and spent at least an hour with him each time. At first there was no change but eventually I managed to get him outside in his wheelchair. We would then push around the hospital, and I even managed to persuade him to get onto a bus. My best success was when I stopped a motorist outside the hospital and asked the driver if he would kindly allow my friend to try and get into his car. The understanding and sympathetic motorist allowed my most audacious request and after much grunting, groaning and even tears, Bill finally managed to get his

Bill, the amputee.

cumbersome frame into the front passenger seat. After this, there was no turning back. Bill improved immensely and in no time he was discharged to return to his family. Sadly, Bill later died during a visit to his home in America.

The culmination of my most eventful year was Matron and I attending the Royal Marines' Christmas Ball at Lympstone. The wonderful evening brought to an end one of the most memorable years of my life. The fact that my endeavours are for the sole purpose of helping others eases my ongoing and persistent burden of grief, which just will *not* go away! It is often said that 'time heals', and maybe it sometimes does, but in my case the feeling of grief still remains. It does, however, have a 'double' effect as it maintains my strong and rigid determination to carry on my fight to hopefully one day bring about a cure for the dreaded cancer.

Although I don't have a 'social calendar' as such, each year my diary seem to fill with all sorts of engagements. The year 2006 too, was to be no exception. From early January, I attended various venues to give my talks and Matron and I were invited to the Mayor's parlour in Wirral and Liverpool. I attended at the number one District Police Training School at Bruche near Warrington, Cheshire with my friend and ex-police colleague Mr Mal Thory. As well as giving an illustrated address to the centre's packed lecture hall, Mal and I also took part in the training schedule by engaging in 'role play' during training lessons. Mal and I have continued being involved in police training at numerous venues ever since.

In March I travelled down to the Marines Training Centre and completed a gruelling '30 miler' with Hunter Company, which not only assisted the recovery of those striving to regain their fitness, but the event raised funds for a Royal Marines charity. A week later I was down with the children at Littlehampton and Worthing taking part in various activities to boost the coffers of the Enable Me charity. On Sunday 23rd April I took part in a very hard and extremely demanding cross country push alongside members of the Cheshire Yeomanry. The event was the brain child of an ex-member Mr Trevor Parry. It was hard for me personally because it was only meant for 'able bodied' people; the course meandered along narrow, muddy footpaths, over stiles as well as negotiating steep muddy hills and a ploughed field. It was truly a wheelchair nightmare! However, my mission was successfully completed and a lot of money was raised for the Children of Chernobyl Charity. I was pleased to have taken part in an endeavour to assist such an extremely worthy cause. After more talking engagements had passed, I went over to Liverpool to push ten miles from Walton Hospital to Alder Hey children's hospital to raise money for the latter's 'Imagine' children's appeal, another worthy and very important cause for sick children. I gave a talk to members of the Unilever staff for the same appeal and received the astronomical sum of £500 for my effort.

My next Royal Marines engagement 'killed two birds with one stone'! I attended various schools down in Worthing and Littlehampton and during my period down there I joined a contingent of Royal Marines at Arundel Castle, the home of my friend Georgina, the Duchess of Norfolk. The purpose of our visit was to abseil down the outside of one of the castle's 150ft towers. This time our goal was to raise funds for the 'Winston's Wish' charity. This is a very important cause as its purpose is to help bereaved children and young people rebuild their lives after a family death. The charity offers practical support and guidance to families, professionals and anyone concerned about a grieving child. This wheelchair abseil was different from my previous 135ft lighthouse drop, as this time I had to be lifted onto the top of the battlements and virtually pushed over the side! I had a freefall drop of ten feet before I took control of my 'hairy' descent. All went well however, and I eventually reached the safety of 'Terra Firma' into the arms of my awaiting Marine colleagues. This event raised over £15,000 to swell the coffers of the very worthy Winston's Wish fund.

On 26th May I attended a very sad event with a friend and ex-Liverpool City Police colleague, Mal Thory. This was the 'Final Parade' to be held at the closing down of the Police Training Centre at Bruche. Once again, those in authority, those faceless wonders in the corridors of power have brought about the demise of what many consider an essential establishment. What was formally the number one District Police Training School has finally been closed down. This academy of police excellence has trained police officers to an extremely high standard of professional excellence for over 60 years. However, due to more bureaucratic 'wisdom' by those bungling and interfering 'Jobsworths' of the Chairbourne Infantry, a most senseless decision was reached in the name of 'economy'! I, like thousands of other police officers, attended Bruche for my initial training which prepared us for the dangers and traumas of

150ft Arundel Castle abseil.

patrolling Britain's angry and dangerous streets. We were taught law to a very high standard, first aid, how to deliver babies (I was to deliver three during my career), unarmed combat and the skills of diplomacy. Each individual officer was instilled with the utmost confidence, enabling them to use their own discretion, initiative and common sense when having to deal with any scenario. The ultimate blow to many hard working and dedicated officers came on 26th May, even though approximately 86,000 police officers have been trained at Bruche over 60 years. The Chairbourne Infantry decided that it would be better if the purpose built, prestigious, elite and extremely efficient Police Academy were to close down. They

Mal Thory.

deemed it more economical to have each force train its own officers! Due to this wisdom of those upstairs, on one of the saddest days of my life, a very wet and windy Friday dawned. I and hundreds of equally sad and disbelieving, past and serving officers of all ranks attended the centre's final parade. I think the establishment will one day regret their ridiculous decision to close such an extremely valuable asset to our increasingly crime ridden country.

June saw a return to Littlehampton and Worthing. This time my daughter Jo accompanied me and we flew from Liverpool to Southampton to be collected by Ann Stimpson, one of the Enable Me Trustees who drove us to our accommodation at Marine Court.

Final parade at the closure of Bruche Police Training Centre.

Our four-day programme included many school visits where I gave talks to the children and also took part in art lessons with them.

One day whilst I was pushing along the roads of Wirral, a lady motorist stopped and told me her daughter had not stopped talking about an illustrated address I gave at her school some time earlier. The lady, Mrs Kenny, asked if I would take part in a 'concert' her ten year old daughter Joanne would like to give to help me raise funds for the Alder Hey Imagine Appeal. I told her I would be delighted to assist in any way I could. Consequently, young Joanne, the ten year old enterprising musician, together with her friends organised a charity 'concert' at Our Lady of Pity church hall in Greasby, Wirral in early August. On the day of the concert the hall was filled to capacity. All the children played beautifully, and some were extremely versatile by playing a number of instruments. One girl performed a beautiful ballet dance to the music of her ten year old friends. I too gave a musical rendition on my chromatic harmonica! It was a breathtaking and really heart–warming performance by a group of very talented youngsters. This very thoughtful and enterprising endeavour by children so young raised the magnificent sum of £600 on the day. However, this was increased by later donations due to following press publicity which resulted in a grand total of £1,000. This massive contribution to such an important cause was brought about in its entirety by the benevolent actions of those caring and talented young children.

By now I had completed another mega effort; I had completed my sixth book, an adventurous and illustrated chronology of my wheelchair push from John O'Groats to Land's End. The book, *Tip to Toe* was successfully published and on Wednesday 23rd August, Matron and I met my publisher, Jeremy Mills, and his charming wife Adriane down at Land's End. As well as Dame Tanni Grey-Thompson writing a very impressive foreword, my book is blessed by endorsements from my two friends The Duchess of Norfolk and Falklands hero Simon Weston. The launch was attended by senior fire officer, ADO Brian Crowle, the police, local dignitaries and officials from the Land's End to John O'Groats Company, as well as the ever present (and much appreciated) press and radio. The book was officially launched from an open air stand in the tiny Land's End 'village'. In no time I was happily signing copies to people visiting the resort from every place imaginable. I met people from my home area of Wirral and Liverpool who were down there on holiday. There were others from foreign lands who purchased my book to take back to their home countries far away across the oceans. Needless to say, Jeremy too was very pleased with the highly successful launch. Jeremy very kindly gave a substantial donation to my cancer charity via the book sales on that day.

A nurse by the name of Mrs Elaine Davies asked if I would assist her to introduce a charity walk in aid of disability awareness. This would be a seven-mile walk from Clatterbridge Hospital back to Elaine's Hospital at Arrowe Park. A lot of extremely hard work was put into this endeavour by Elaine and her hospital colleagues to bring her idea to successful fruition. I assisted the raising of funds via my 'after dinner' talks and together, Elaine and her 'gang' with yours truly in tow set off from Clatterbridge Hospital in September. Those taking part included nurses, their families and friends, patients and a fire and ambulance service escort during our lengthy walk. On arrival at Arrowe Park we were met by the Mayor of Wirral and the press. The walk raised over £3,000 and I am exceedingly grateful to all who took part and gave so generously to such a worthy cause. It was a privilege to have been in such wonderful company as those enterprising and wonderful 'Florence Nightingales'.

My continued talks and pushes and visits to Lympstone and Worthing brought yet another year to a close. I paraded at the Wallasey War Memorial with the Royal Marines Cadet unit on 11th November proudly wearing my green 'lid' and gongs, representing Hunter Company, Royal Marines, Lympstone. Although over nine long years have passed since my amputation, the same length of time is but a brief period regarding the loss of my dear wife Marje and the pain does not wane. I continue with my deep and proud involvement with the children of Enable Me, and my persevering efforts will relentlessly persist to improve conditions for the disabled fraternity. I do concede that the UK is starting to get to grips with the extremely out of date way a lot of people still behave. Sadly the 'does he take sugar' syndrome still very much prevails throughout all walks (forgive the pun) of our so-called modern, welfare-orientated and concerned society. This scenario will not be eliminated until much more is done. However, it is the children and youth of the country who are without doubt educating the adult population as to awareness of mental and physical disability. I still encounter thoughtless individuals who curse and swear because wheelchair users have to request things like a door to be opened to allow wheelchairs into a shop, café or other similar premises.

I experienced such an incident recently when I had to mount a high pavement, and then attempt to mount a step to get into a shop only to find that one of the two doors would not open. The other door was locked and bolted shut so the gap offered by the one open door was too narrow for my chair to get through. When I finally attracted the attention of one of the female shop assistants, her disdain was obvious. As it was windy and raining, the rain was blowing into the shop and I was actually admonished for 'allowing the cold into the shop'! Only recently when Matron and I were dining in a hotel in the evening a head waiter whispered into Matron's ear, 'We can put him into a side room in the morning and that will make more room at breakfast'! I can't even put into writing what the gist of Matron's dulcet reply to the offending buffoon was. When booking into a hotel, the pen is always offered to whoever I am with but not to me. Perhaps they think I will scribble all over the walls. Many times when I pay for items while out shopping with Matron or my daughter, if there is any change this is nearly *always* handed to whoever I am with instead of me. This is no doubt to prevent me from putting the money into my mouth! Another offensive form of behaviour manifests itself when I am being dealt with at a shop counter, when someone suddenly pushes in front of me or leans over me demanding to be served as they are in a hurry. Many times when I am engaged in conversation in the company of others, those present talk across the top of me as though I am a child butting into in adult conversation. The example set by the a fifth year student of Davison High School in bringing about the Enable Me project is an example of just how much some *do* care – who says youngsters don't care nowadays?

As my fundraising endeavours go on, so does my continual monitoring and assessing of facilities offered by the authorities towards the disabled. I am *more* than willing to assist any authorities, local councils or other bodies to bring about the bettering and understanding which will enhance disability awareness. My enthusiastic, eccentric yet obsessive crusade will continue on, and hopefully one day the dreaded scourge of cancer may be either eliminated, or a cure may be found. There are many other worthy causes I will continue to assist also, and nothing will deter my ongoing efforts, as these are all carried out in memory of and for...... the love of Marje.